Arizona Legal Research

Carolina Academic Press
Legal Research Series

Suzanne E. Rowe, Series Editor

ﻉ

Arizona — Tamara S. Herrera

Arkansas — Coleen M. Barger

Florida, Third Edition — Barbara J. Busharis & Suzanne E. Rowe

Georgia — Nancy P. Johnson, Elizabeth G. Adelman, & Nancy J. Adams

Idaho — Tenielle Fordyce-Ruff & Suzanne E. Rowe

Illinois — Mark E. Wojcik

Michigan — Pamela Lysaght

Missouri — Wanda M. Temm & Julie M. Cheslik

Oregon, Second Edition — Suzanne E. Rowe

Pennsylvania — Barbara J. Busharis & Bonny L. Tavares

Tennessee — Sibyl Marshall & Carol McCrehan Parker

Washington — Julie Heintz

ﻉ

Arizona Legal Research

Tamara S. Herrera
Sandra Day O'Connor College of Law
Arizona State University

Suzanne E. Rowe, Series Editor

CAROLINA ACADEMIC PRESS
Durham, North Carolina

Library of Congress Cataloging-in-Publication Data

Herrera, Tamara.
Arizona legal research / by Tamara Herrera.
    p. cm. -- (Legal research series)
Includes bibliographical references and index.
ISBN 978-1-59460-354-9 (alk. paper)
1. Legal research--Arizona. I. Title.
KFA2475.H47 2008
340.072'0791--dc22

                                                    2007048761

CAROLINA ACADEMIC PRESS
700 Kent Street
Durham, North Carolina 27701
Telephone (919) 489-7486
Fax (919) 493-5668
www.cap-press.com

Printed in the United States of America.

Summary of Contents

Contents

List of Tables

Series Note

The Legal Research Series published by Carolina Academic Press includes an increasing number of titles from states around the country. The goal of each book is to provide law students, practitioners, paralegals, college students, and laypeople with the essential elements of legal research in each state. Unlike more bibliographic texts, the Legal Research Series books seek to explain concisely both the sources of state law research and the process for conducting legal research effectively.

Acknowledgments

I owe a great debt of gratitude to Suzanne Rowe, series editor, for her support of this project. She generously provided both her time and her material for Chapter 1 and Appendix A, for which I am grateful.

I also owe many thanks to others who supported me throughout this project with advice and materials: specifically, Marianne Alcorn, Kirsten Davis, Beth DiFelice, Amy Langenfeld, Chad Noreuil, Sigmund Popko, Judith Stinson, and Connie Strittmatter. Both the Ross-Blakely Law Library staff and the legal writing department at the Sandra Day O'Connor College of Law (Arizona State University) are composed of wonderfully talented individuals. The law school simply could not function without them, and they are the best colleagues one could hope for in any job.

In addition, no acknowledgement would be complete without thanking my parents, Thom and Carol Havelaar, for their support of all my writing projects, from the first book review I wrote at the age of twelve that they lovingly tucked in the pages of a scrapbook to all of my current work.

Finally, my greatest thanks go to my husband, William, and my son, Eric, for understanding my need to write and reminding me why life is beautiful.

Arizona Legal Research

Chapter 1

The Research Process

I. Arizona Legal Research

The fundamentals of legal research are the same in every American jurisdiction, though the details vary. While some variations are minor, others require specialized knowledge of the resources available. This book focuses on the resources required to be thorough and effective in researching Arizona law. It supplements this focus with brief explanations of federal research, Arizona tribal law research, and research into the law of other states, both to introduce other resources and to highlight some of the variations.

II. The Intersection of Legal Research and Legal Analysis

Most students realize in the first week of law school that legal analysis is difficult. At the same time, some consider legal research simplistic busy work. The basic process of legal research *is* simple. For most print resources, a legal researcher will begin with an index, find entries that appear relevant, read those sections of the text, and then find out whether more recent information is available. For most online research, a researcher will search particular websites or databases using words likely to appear in the text of relevant documents.

Legal analysis is interwoven throughout this process, raising challenging questions. In print research, which words should be looked up in the index? How does one decide whether an index entry looks promising? With online research, how does one choose relevant words and construct a search most likely to produce the needed documents? When reading the text of a document, how does one determine whether it is relevant to a client's situation? How does one learn whether more recent material changed the law or merely applied it in a new situation? The answer to each of these questions requires legal analysis. This intersection of research and analysis can make this process very difficult, especially for the novice.

This book is not designed to be a blueprint of every resource in the law library or search engine on the Internet; many resources contain their own detailed explanations in a preface or a "Help" section. This book is more like a manual or field guide, introducing the resources needed at each step of the research process and explaining how to use them. Legal researchers will find the book most helpful if they read it in the library, where they can refer to the sources discussed, or near a computer connected to the Internet.

III. Types of Legal Authority

Before researching the law, be clear about the goal of the search. In every research situation, the goal is to find constitutional provisions, statutes, administrative rules, and judicial opinions that control the client's situation. In other words, search for primary, mandatory authority.

Law is often divided along two lines. The first line distinguishes primary authority from secondary authority. *Primary authority* is law produced by government bodies with law-making power. Legislatures write statutes; courts write judicial opinions; and administrative agencies write rules (also called regulations). *Secondary authority* includes all other legal sources, such as treatises, law review articles, and legal encyclopedias. These secondary sources are designed to aid a legal researcher in understanding the law and locating primary authority.

Another division is made between mandatory and persuasive authority. *Mandatory authority* is binding on the court that would de-

Table 1-1. Examples of Authority in Arizona Research

	Mandatory Authority	Persuasive Authority
Primary Authority	Arizona Constitution Arizona statutes Arizona rules Arizona Supreme Court cases	California statutes Nevada rules New Mexico Supreme Court cases
Secondary Authority		Treatises Law review articles Legal encyclopedias

cide a conflict if the situation were litigated. In a question of Arizona law, mandatory authority includes Arizona's constitution, statutes enacted by the Arizona legislature, opinions of the Arizona Supreme Court,[1] and Arizona administrative rules. *Persuasive authority* is not binding but may be followed if it is relevant and well reasoned. Authority may be merely persuasive if it is from a different jurisdiction or if it is not produced by a law-making body. In a question of Arizona law, examples of persuasive authority include a similar California statute, an opinion of a New Mexico state court, and a law review article. Notice in Table 1-1 that persuasive authority may be either primary or secondary authority, while mandatory authority is always primary authority.

Within primary, mandatory authority, there is an interlocking hierarchy of law involving constitutions, statutes, administrative rules, and judicial opinions. The constitution of each state is the supreme law of that state. If a statute is on point, that statute comes next in the hierarchy, followed by administrative rules. Judicial opinions may interpret statutes or rules but cannot disregard them. A judicial opinion may, however, decide that a statute violates the constitution or that a rule oversteps its bounds. If there is no constitutional provi-

---

1. An opinion from the Arizona Court of Appeals is binding on the trial courts if the Arizona Supreme Court has not addressed a particular topic.

sion, statute, or administrative rule on point, the issue will be controlled by *common law* (also called judge-made law).

IV. Court Systems

Because much legal research includes reading judicial opinions, legal researchers need to understand the court system. The basic court structure includes a trial court, an intermediate court of appeals, and an ultimate appellate court, often called the "supreme" court.[2] These courts exist at both the state and federal levels.

A. Arizona Courts

In Arizona, the general jurisdiction trial court is called the Arizona Superior Court. The Arizona Superior Court has locations in each of Arizona's fifteen counties. The smaller counties have only one judge, while the larger counties have more than one judge. In the larger counties, the judges are divided into numbered divisions. Generally, counties with more than one judge have a juvenile division. In addition, the Maricopa County Superior Court has the Tax Court, which hears all tax cases in Arizona.

Arizona's intermediate court is called the Arizona Court of Appeals. This court has two divisions: Division One in Phoenix and Division Two in Tucson. Division One has sixteen judges, and Division Two has six judges. The Arizona Court of Appeals judges sit in three-judge panels and hear appeals from the Arizona Superior Court; Division One also hears appeals from the Industrial Commission, the Department of Economic Security, and the Tax Court.

---

2. The following description omits for brevity Arizona's Justice of the Peace Courts and Municipal Courts, which are limited jurisdiction courts. Basic information about these courts is available online through a variety of websites. Arizona tribal courts are addressed later in Chapter 9.

The Arizona Supreme Court, which sits in Phoenix, has five justices.[3] The five justices sit *en banc* to hear all cases, unless a justice is recused. The Arizona Supreme Court hears all death penalty cases in Arizona and has the discretion to review cases from the Arizona Court of Appeals when a party files a petition for review. The website for the Arizona Judicial Branch is www.supreme.state .az.us. It contains a wealth of information, including a map of Arizona court locations, the Guide to Arizona Courts, links to Arizona courts maintaining websites, links to Arizona Revised Statutes and Arizona Rules of Court, links to self-service court forms, and links to the recent opinions of both the Arizona Court of Appeals and the Arizona Supreme Court. The site also provides a free listserve function, which automatically notifies registrants when the Arizona Supreme Court releases a new opinion or administrative order.

B. Federal Courts

In the federal judicial system, the trial courts are called United States District Courts. There are ninety-four district courts in the federal system, with each district drawn from a particular state. A state with a relatively small population may not be subdivided into smaller geographic regions. The entire state of Arizona, for example, makes up the federal District of Arizona. Even so, district courts are located in two cities: Phoenix and Tucson. States with larger populations and higher caseloads are subdivided into more districts. For example, California has four federal districts: northern, central, southern, and eastern.

Intermediate appellate courts in the federal system are called United States Courts of Appeals. There are courts of appeals for each of the thirteen federal circuits. Twelve of these circuits are based on geographic jurisdiction. In addition to eleven numbered circuits cov-

---

3. A jurist on the highest court is called a "justice" while on lower courts the term "judge" is used.

ering all the states, there is the District of Columbia Circuit. The thirteenth federal circuit, called the Federal Circuit, hears appeals from district courts in all other circuits on issues related to patent law and from certain specialized courts and agencies. A map showing the federal circuits is available at www.uscourts.gov/courtlinks. Circuit maps may also be found in the front of *Federal Supplement* and *Federal Reporter*, books that publish the cases decided by federal courts.

Arizona is in the Ninth Circuit. This means that cases from the United States District Court for the District of Arizona are appealed to the United States Court of Appeals for the Ninth Circuit. This circuit encompasses Alaska, Arizona, California, Hawaii, Idaho, Montana, Nevada, Oregon, and Washington, as well as Guam and the Northern Mariana Islands.

The highest court in the federal system is the United States Supreme Court. It decides cases concerning the United States Constitution and federal statutes. This court does not have the final say on matters of purely state law; that authority rests with the highest court of each state. Parties who wish to have the United States Supreme Court hear their case must file a *petition for certiorari*, as the court has discretion over which cases it hears.

The website for the federal judiciary contains maps, court addresses, explanations of jurisdiction, and other helpful information. The address is www.uscourts.gov.

C. Courts of Other States

Most states have the three-tier court system of Arizona and the federal judiciary. A few states do not have an intermediate appellate court. Another difference in some court systems is that the "supreme" court is not the highest court. In New York, the trial courts are called supreme courts, and the highest court is the Court of Appeals. Two other states, Massachusetts and Maine, call their highest court the Supreme Judicial Court.

Citation manuals are good references for learning the names and hierarchy of the courts, as well as for learning proper citation to legal authorities. The two most popular are the *ALWD Citation Manual: A Professional System of Citation,* written by Dean Darby Dickerson and the Association of Legal Writing Directors,[4] and *The Bluebook: A Uniform System of Citation,* written by students from several law schools.[5] Appendix 1 of the *ALWD Manual* and Table 1 of the *Bluebook* provide information on federal and state courts.

V. Overview of the Research Process

Conducting effective legal research means following a process. This process leads to the authority that controls a legal issue as well as to commentary that may help a legal researcher analyze new and complex legal matters. The outline in Table 1-2 presents the basic research process.

This basic process should be customized for each research project. Consider whether all seven steps need to be followed, and if so, in what order. If an area of law is unfamiliar, follow each step of the process in the order indicated. Beginning with secondary sources will provide both context for the issues and citations to relevant primary authority. After gaining experience in a certain area, a legal researcher may modify the process as needed. For example, a legal researcher who knows that a situation is controlled by a statute may choose to begin with Step 3.

A. Generating Research Terms

Many legal resources in print use lengthy indexes as the starting point for finding legal authority. Electronic media often require the legal researcher to enter words that are likely to appear in a synopsis

---

4. ALWD & Darby Dickerson, *ALWD Citation Manual* (3d ed., Aspen 2006) ("*ALWD Manual*"). Most citations in this book conform to the *ALWD Manual.*

5. *The Bluebook: A Uniform System of Citation* (The Columbia Law Review et al. eds., 18th ed., The Harvard Law Review Assn. 2005).

Table 1-2. Overview of the Research Process

Step 1: Determine the *issue* and generate a list of *research terms.*

Step 2: Consult *secondary sources* and practice aids. For basic background information, consult legal encyclopedias, treatises, and dictionaries. For more specific issues or cutting-edge areas of the law, consult law review articles and the *American Law Reports.*

Step 3: Find controlling *constitutional provisions, statutes,* or *rules* by searching their indexes in print or searching their full text or indexes online for the research terms, then reading the relevant sections. Also record citations to relevant cases that may be referenced.

Step 4: Use *digests* or *online case finding tools* to find citations to cases. A digest is essentially a multi-volume topic index of cases in a certain jurisdiction or subject area.

Step 5: Read the cases in *reporters* or in an *online database.* A reporter series publishes the full text of cases in a certain jurisdiction or subject area.

Step 6: *Update* or "Shepardize" the legal authorities to ensure they have not been repealed, reversed, modified, or otherwise changed.

Step 7: *Stop* research when research in various sources no longer produces new legal authorities and when no analytical holes remain.

or in the full text of relevant documents. To ensure thoroughness in beginning a research project, start with a comprehensive list of words, terms, and phrases that may lead to law on point. These may be legal terms or common words that describe the client's situation. The items on this list are *research terms.*

Organized brainstorming is the best way to compile a comprehensive list of research terms. Some legal researchers ask the journalistic questions: Who? What? How? Why? When? Where? Others use a mnemonic device like TARPP, which stands for Things, Actions, Remedies, People, and Places.[6] Whether using one of these sugges-

---

6. *See* Roy M. Mersky & Donald J. Dunn, *Fundamentals of Legal Research* 15 (8th ed., Found. Press 2002) (explaining "TARP," a similar mnemonic device).

tions or developing an individual method, generate a broad range of research terms regarding the facts, issues, and desired solutions of the client's situation. Include in the list both specific and general words. Try to think of synonyms and antonyms for each term since at this point there is uncertainty which terms an index may include.

As an example, consider the following case of a family law attorney. The attorney's newest client divorced her husband three years ago, and after the trial court entered the decree she took her husband back to court to modify custody arrangements for their two children. The client had to spend over $3,500 in attorney's fees for the modification, and her ex-husband spent the same amount. The trial court ordered the client to pay her ex-husband's fees because the client makes $100,000 per year as a business executive while her ex-husband is unemployed. The client wants to know if she has an obligation to pay her ex-husband's fees. Table 1-3 provides examples of research terms the attorney might use to begin work on this project.

As the research project progresses, the attorney will learn new research terms to include in the list and decide to take others off. For example, reading cases may give some insights into the key words

Table 1-3. Generating Research Terms

Journalistic Approach

Who:	husband, wife, spouse, trial court, judge
What:	attorney fees, fees, costs, money
How:	decree, order, change
Why:	modification, change, custody, children
When:	post-divorce
Where:	trial court, court

TARPP Approach

Things:	order, custody, divorce, children
Actions:	change, modify
Remedies:	pay, fees, attorney fees, costs, money
People:	husband, wife, spouse, judge, attorney
Places:	trial court, court

judges tend to use in discussing this topic. Or there may be a *term of art*, a word or phrase that has special meaning in this particular area of law. These need to be added to the list.

B. Selecting Print or Electronic Media

In a perfect world, a legal researcher could choose whether to conduct research in print media or electronic media without consideration as to time, cost, or even ease of use. Since the reality is that research costs, both in time and money, it is generally important to choose a research media that is the most cost-effective. The first question in determining the most cost-effective research media is to ask whether there are any limitations on the research. This may be a helpful question to ask the attorney assigning the research project or the client. For example, it is not uncommon for some clients to refuse to pay for research conducted on pay research databases, such as Lexis-Nexis or Westlaw. Always know how much time and money can be spent on a research project before beginning to research.

The second question in determining the most cost-effective research media is to ask what resources the office has available for use. An office may have print media, electronic media, or both. Generally, cost-effective media include print media, free Internet sources, or pay research databases that charge a special rate for their use.[7] For example, it would not make sense to log on to LexisNexis or Westlaw and pay a fee to copy an Arizona statute if the office has copies of *Arizona Revised Statutes Annotated* available for use. Never pay for a research task that can easily be done for free or for a minimal cost.

---

7. Even if an office pays one flat rate for access to research databases such as LexisNexis and Westlaw, it is important to use those databases in a cost-effective manner. Generally, when an office is negotiating for a renewal of a flat rate contract, it will have to pay a new flat rate based on prior, actual use of the database.

The third question in determining the most cost-effective research media is to consider what general type of research is being done. Some projects are better suited for research using print media, while other projects are better suited for research using electronic media. On the one hand, issues that involve common terms or broad subjects, such as procedural issues, are generally easier to research using print media. On the other hand, issues that involve specific facts, comparisons of laws, or current legal events are generally easier to research using electronic media. In addition, when checking whether a case or statute is still good law, it is best to use an electronic-media citator, which will be more up-to-date and more readily available than any print citator.

If electronic pay databases are the most cost-effective choices for research, consider how to use them most efficiently. There are two important considerations: (1) choice of database and (2) choice of pricing structure. First, in choosing a database, it is most effective — as to time and cost — to choose the narrowest database that will give relevant results. This is because larger databases, such as "Federal and State Cases, Combined" in LexisNexis and "ALLCASES" in Westlaw, cost more money to use in an hourly pricing structure. Larger databases may also yield a larger number of results, which will take longer to read and assess.

Next, if an office does not have a flat rate fee structure for LexisNexis or Westlaw, it will have one or both of the following pricing structures: hourly and transactional. Hourly pricing charges based on how many minutes the researcher is logged on to the database. Transactional pricing charges for the number of searches that the researcher performs. If using transactional pricing, it is important to draft a word search before entering the word search into the pay research database. It also cost-effective to draft a word search as broadly as possible to retrieve the greatest number of cases, because transactional pricing does not charge for a restrictive search within a results list.[8]

---

8. Section V.C below explains how to use the sub-search functions "FOCUS" in LexisNexis and "Locate" in Westlaw.

C. Composing a Word Search for Electronic Media

Although electronic media allow searching with one word, this one-word search may not be narrow enough to retrieve relevant results. In this case, a comprehensive word search can be constructed either in natural language or with Boolean terms and connectors.

Most legal researchers are familiar with natural language searches. These are the word searches used on many websites, including Google. A *natural language* search is simply a question typed into the website's or database's search engine.[9] A natural language search will not produce an exhaustive list of relevant sources, but it will likely produce one good source upon which to base further research. Thus, natural language searching is a good first step if the researcher is uncertain what words or phrases would appear in a relevant source.

With some certainty about what words or phrases would appear in a relevant source, it is best to start with Boolean searching. A *Boolean search* involves the use of specific connectors and commands to tell the search engine how the words and phrases should appear in a relevant source. Using a Boolean search allows more control over the search engine's search process. The best way to construct an effective Boolean search is to first consider what the ideal relevant source would look like: What words and phrases would it include? Where would these words and phrases appear? Table 1-4 explains the most common Boolean connectors and commands.

Using the connectors and commands from Table 1-4, searching the terms: *(covenant or contract) /p (noncompetition or compet!) /p employ!*, the computer will look for:

- either the term *covenant* or *contract*
- within the same paragraph as the term *noncompetition* or variations *of competition, compete, competitor*
- and also in that paragraph, variations of *employ, employee, employer, employment.*

---

9. Choose this option directly on the search screen by clicking the appropriate tab or radio button.

Misuse of Boolean connectors can produce bizarre search results. If, instead of "/p" behind the first set of parentheses in the example above the legal researcher used the "or" connector, the results could include a patent case for a popular drug used to prevent respiratory tract disease in infants, an antitrust case against a telephone company/Internet provider, and a Deceptive Trade Practices Act case against a cigarette manufacturer for labeling cigarettes "light."

In some cases, a word search may return too many results to read. Both LexisNexis and Westlaw have functions to narrow these results without restarting the research process. This function is called

Table 1-4. Boolean Connectors and Commands

Goal	LexisNexis	Westlaw
To find alternative terms anywhere in the document	or	or blank space
To find both terms anywhere in the document	and &	and &
To find both terms within a particular distance from each other	/p=within same paragraph /s=within same sentence /n=within a certain number of words (n=choice of number)	/p=within same paragraph /s=within same sentence /n=within a certain number of words (n=choice of number)
To find terms used as a phrase	leave a blank space between each word of the phrase	put the phrase in quotation marks
To control the hierarchy of searching	parentheses	parentheses
To exclude terms	and not	but not %
To extend the end of the term	!	!
To hold the place of letters in a term	*	*

"FOCUS" in LexisNexis and "Locate" in Westlaw. By choosing this function from the search results list, a legal researcher can conduct a second search. This second search then reviews only the results from the initial search. In short, this function allows a legal researcher to search within a search.

D. Choosing a Starting Point for Research

After assessing which research materials are the most cost-effective to use, assess at which point in the process to begin the research. Although research is rarely a linear process, there is an effective method for researching a project, as shown in Table 1-2. Generally, this method requires beginning with secondary sources both to gain familiarity with the area of law being researched and to find citations to primary law. The next step is to determine if a constitution or statute is involved in answering the research question; at this stage, also determine if international law, administrative law, or legislative history is involved in answering the research question.

Next, research case law. Then update any primary authority that has been found to determine if that authority is still good law and to find leads to other sources that cite to that primary authority. Repeat this process of updating and looking up new sources until the same sources are mentioned over and over again or until all holes in the legal analysis have been filled. This is a good stopping point, but it does not mean that the research process is over. During the reading and writing process, the legal researcher may find that the sources used may contain citations to other relevant sources, at which point it is necessary to research those sources. It is also possible that a new primary authority will become available (e.g., a court decides a new case on the research issue), and this authority may need to be incorporated into the legal analysis. Legal research is only done when the final product of the research project is done.

Not every research project needs to follow the research method set forth in Table 1-2. Many research projects have a specific place to start because they contain some information about an applicable source of primary authority. This information can be a constitution, statutory, or case citation, or a constitution, statutory, or case name. If this information exists, start the research project using this information, as it is possible to go back later and research other sources of primary law that may be helpful.

E. Other Helpful Hints

Keep good notes during the research. These notes should indicate what sources have been searched and when these sources were last searched, as well as any research terms and findings. These notes will be helpful if the research project is interrupted. These notes may also be helpful if someone asks for a log of what has been done on a research project.

Know the office librarian. Librarians are experts in research and can offer help if there is no clear starting point for the research, if the research has hit a roadblock, or if it is hard to know when to stop researching. For these same reasons, it is also important to get to know the local librarians at the nearest law school or county law library.

F. Researching the Law—Organization of This Text

The remainder of this book explains how to conduct legal research in a variety of sources. Chapter 2 addresses how to use secondary sources and practice aids to locate primary authority, which is the ultimate goal of legal research. Chapter 3 addresses the Arizona Constitution, which is the highest legal authority in the state. Chapter 4 describes statutory research, while Chapter 5 describes legislative history. Chapters 6 and 7 explain how to use reporters and digests, and their online equivalents, to research judicial decisions. Chapter 8 addresses administrative law, and Chapter 9 addresses Arizona tribal law research. Chapter 10 explains how to update legal authority, which is the process that legal researchers use to ensure that a statute or case is still good law and currently in effect; updating also allows legal researchers to locate other authority relating to the statute or case they are updating. Each of these chapters includes explanations of how to conduct both print and online legal research and provides relevant website addresses for online research.

Adding to this discussion, Appendix A provides an overview of the conventions lawyers follow in citing legal authority in their documents. Appendix B contains a glossary of legal research terms used in this book.

VI. Rules Governing Attorney Conduct

Conducting effective research is an important part of an attorney's role in assisting clients. The Arizona Ethics Rules[10] cover all aspects of legal practice. Rule 1.1 states, "A lawyer shall provide competent representation to a client. Competent representation requires the legal knowledge, skill, thoroughness and preparation reasonably necessary for the representation." A large part of this knowledge and preparation comes from legal research. This book provides instruction in how to conduct effective and efficient research into Arizona law.

---

10. Arizona Rules of Professional Conduct, also commonly referred to as Arizona Ethics Rules, are available in *Arizona Revised Statutes Annotated* and *Arizona Rules of Court: State.* The rules are also available on the Arizona State Bar's website at www.myazbar.org/ethics/rules.cfm.

Chapter 2

Researching Secondary Authority

Consider beginning any legal research project by looking at secondary authority. Secondary authority may be helpful in two scenarios: (1) when researching an unfamiliar or undeveloped area of law or (2) when trying to locate primary authority if there are no solid leads to follow. Some benefits of using secondary authority include that many are written in easy-to-understand plain English and that many provide citations to, and explanations of, primary authority. In other words, someone else has done some of the research.

Although consulting a secondary authority is a good first step in a legal research project, this is by no means the only time in a legal research project that a secondary authority will be helpful. Legal research is rarely a purely linear activity. Many times reading a statute or case will raise additional issues for research. The most effective way to begin researching the new issues may be to return to a secondary source. Thus, use secondary authority throughout the legal research process, depending on the complexity of the issues.

For basic background information and general issues, it is best to consult legal encyclopedias, treatises, and dictionaries. For more specific issues or cutting-edge areas of the law, it is best to consult legal periodicals, *American Law Reports*, and *Restatements of Law*. State-specific secondary sources and practice aids are good starting points for most legal research projects on state law issues.

I. Arizona Secondary Sources and Practice Aids

Arizona, like many jurisdictions, has state-specific secondary sources and practice aids that should be consulted during a state research project. Generally, these sources are authored by distinguished Arizona lawyers and judges. These sources include (1) Continuing Legal Education materials and handbooks, (2) jury instructions, and (3) legal forms.

A. Continuing Legal Education Materials and Handbooks

Arizona has an extensive list of Continuing Legal Education materials available through the State Bar of Arizona. Many of these materials are available in print and on CD-ROM. The list of available Arizona Continuing Legal Education materials is on the State Bar of Arizona's website (for purchase) at www.azbar.org.

Arizona's Continuing Legal Education materials include publications on the following subjects:

Administrative law	Health care/medical
Alternative dispute resolution	Immigration
Animal law	Indian law
Appellate practice	Insurance
Bankruptcy	Intellectual property
Business	Law practice management
Construction law	Litigation
Creditor/debtor law	Mental health and elder law
Criminal law/DUI	Personal injury law
Employment and labor law	Probate and estate planning
Environmental and land use law	Professionalism
Ethics	Tax law
Family law	Workers' compensation

Most law libraries also have print-media copies of these materials, and some of these materials are available on Westlaw's "AZPRAC" database. To check which materials currently are available on Westlaw, click on the "Database Directory" link on the home page to Westlaw and "drill down" or "telescope" through layers of the directory to the entry for "Forms, Treatises, CLEs and Other Practice Materials."

B. Jury Instructions

Jury instructions are helpful research sources even if a case is not in litigation. Jury instructions contain references to relevant Arizona cases and statutes that are included as part of the jury instructions' notes. Arizona's model jury instructions are available in most law libraries, as well as on LexisNexis in the "Arizona Jury Instructions–Civil" database and on Westlaw in the "AZ-JIF-CIV" database.

C. Legal Forms

Legal forms are another great source for starting legal research because not only do they give guidance on the particulars of a legal document, but they may also provide references to relevant Arizona cases and statutes. One important source for Arizona-specific legal forms is the 10-volume series *Arizona Legal Forms*.[1] This series is authored by several distinguished Arizona practitioners. This series and other general legal forms are available in print media in most law libraries and on Westlaw on the "AZ-LF" database.

Arizona courts also have self-service centers that offer legal forms and information. These forms and information are available online at http://supreme.state.az.us/nav2/selfserv.htm.

---

1. *Arizona Legal Forms* (3d ed., Thomson West 2002).

II. Encyclopedias

A legal encyclopedia is organized and presented in a similar manner to general encyclopedias. Specifically, a legal encyclopedia contains an alphabetical listing of legal topics with a general overview of the law for each topic. Ideally, use a legal encyclopedia for background information. Although legal encyclopedias contain some citations to primary authorities, they provide no analysis of those authorities.

The two legal encyclopedias relied on by legal researchers are *American Jurisprudence, Second Edition (Am. Jur. 2d)* and *Corpus Juris Secundum (C.J.S.)*. Most law libraries carry both sets. While some states have legal encyclopedias, Arizona does not.

Using an encyclopedia in print media is a three-step process, as outlined in Table 2-1. First, use the encyclopedia's index to locate the proper legal topic. The index to *Am. Jur. 2d* is located at the end of the set; the same is true for *C.J.S.* A list of research terms is helpful in searching the index for relevant legal topics. In some instances, a legal topic may be sub-divided into smaller discussions and given a section number.

Second, once relevant legal topics and any section numbers are located in the index, locate the legal topics and section numbers in the main encyclopedia volumes by finding the volume in which that topic is published. Then read the relevant section(s) of that topic.

Table 2-1.
Outline of the Research Process in a Print-Media Encyclopedia

Step 1: Generate research terms and use them to look in the encyclopedia index to locate the legal topic(s) and relevant sections.

Step 2: Find the volume of the encyclopedia containing the legal topic(s) and any section number and read the relevant portion of the legal topic(s).

Step 3: Review both the volume's table of contents and any pocket part for additional, relevant information.

Finally, review the organization of that legal topic in the volume's table of contents to see if other sections of the topic may be relevant. Also review the back of the volume to see if there is a pocket part or supplement adding new information on the relevant legal topic or section. *Am. Jur. 2d* is available electronically, as well as in print. LexisNexis provides access to it in the "American Law Reports and American Jurisprudence 2d, Combined" database, and Westlaw provides access to it in the "AMJUR" database. *C.J.S.* is available only on Westlaw in the "CJS" database. In order to research a legal topic in electronic media, there is one basic step. Perform a word search in the full-text database, as explained in Chapter 1, in order to find the relevant legal topic. Alternatively, search the table of contents or index of the encyclopedia.

III. Treatises

A treatise is simply a book about a legal topic. Treatises will generally provide more in-depth coverage of a legal topic than an encyclopedia. In addition, treatises may provide more citations to, and analysis of, primary authority. In some instances, a treatise will be authored by a highly respected expert and could carry some persuasive weight in a legal analysis.

Treatises may contain many volumes, and there may even be several editions of some treatises. If a research project asks for the evolution of a legal topic, using older editions of a treatise will help track the topic's history.

Using a treatise is a straightforward, three-step process. First, locate a treatise in the research area. All law libraries should have an extensive collection of treatises organized by topics. The best way to find a treatise is to use a list of research terms to search the library's catalog or to consult a reference librarian. Next, locate the relevant portion of the treatise. Most treatises provide a table of contents and an index to help with this step.

Finally, read the relevant portions of the treatise and take notes of potentially helpful citations to primary authority. Remember that treatises are rarely available in electronic media and are rarely updated by pocket parts and supplements. Thus, always make note of when a treatise was written to assess whether to find more current sources.

IV. Dictionaries

Never discount the helpfulness of dictionaries. Although they rarely provide citations to primary authority, they will provide easy-to-understand definitions of terms that may be unfamiliar. *Black's Law Dictionary*, published by Thomson West, is the most widely used legal dictionary. All law libraries have copies of it. It is also available on Westlaw in the "BLACKS" database. LexisNexis provides access to other legal dictionaries in its "Legal Dictionaries, Combined" database.

Similarly, never discount the usefulness of non-legal dictionaries and thesauri. A dictionary may provide a useful, easy-to-understand definition of an unknown term. A thesaurus may help expand a list of research terms. Many dictionaries and thesauri are available in law libraries. Good websites to try are:

- www.law.com
- www.dictionaryreference.com
- www.m-w.com
- www.yourdictionary.com.

V. Legal Periodicals

Legal periodicals include many different types of publications: legal newspapers, legal magazines, commercially published law journals, peer-edited law journals, and law-school published law journals (also commonly called law reviews). Generally, legal periodicals include analytical articles on a narrow issue of law or a new area of law. These articles are authored by law professors, practitioners, judges, and sometimes editors. Law students also publish articles in law journals; these articles are called notes or comments, and they generally analyze a case's holding and reasoning in depth. Articles in legal journals are unique because they tend to include detailed background on an issue and a well researched list of citations to primary (and other secondary) authority. Some journal articles, however, simply alert subscribers to new developments in the law, with little analysis of those developments.

The two steps to researching legal periodicals in print media are outlined in Table 2-2. There are two print-media indexes: *Index to Legal Periodicals* and *Current Law Index*. Both indexes are noncumulative in nature, meaning that each volume of the index covers a different period of time. In order to research all published legal periodicals, it is necessary to look in several different volumes of the index.

Both print indexes generally include the same universe of legal periodicals, covering periodicals published from roughly 1980 to the present. Both indexes are organized alphabetically by legal topic. Search the index for research terms, which will lead to a relevant legal topic. After locating a relevant legal topic, note the citations to applicable legal periodicals following the topic heading. One difference between the two indexes is organization of author information. *Current Law Index* contains a separate index of authors, while *Index to Legal Periodicals* includes authors' names as part of the subject index.

Because noncumulative volumes are time-consuming to research, most law libraries have legal periodical indexes available on their electronic catalogs. A law library's electronic catalog may include the electronic version of *Index to Legal Periodicals* or another index called *LegalTrac*. *LegalTrac* is useful because, in addition to citing legal periodicals, it includes citations to law-related articles from general pe-

Table 2-2.
Outline of the Research Process in a Print-Media Legal Periodical

Step 1: Generate research terms and use them to look in an index (*Index to Legal Periodicals, Current Law Index, LegalTrac,* HeinOnline) to locate citations to relevant legal periodicals.

Step 2: Find the legal periodical using the citation and read the legal periodical.

Table 2-3.
Selected LexisNexis and Westlaw Databases for Legal Periodicals

LexisNexis Databases	Westlaw Databases
Law Reviews, CLE, Legal Journals & Periodicals, Combined	TP-ALL (all law reviews, texts, articles)
US Law Reviews & Journals, Combined	JLR (law journal articles only)
Law Reviews and ALR	

riodicals.[2] To search either electronic index, use a keyword or author search. A search will result in a list of citations that can be taken to the law library's shelves to locate the specific articles. In some instances, the indexes may also provide the full text of an article, depending on the library's subscription agreement. Like the print indexes, these electronic indexes cover periodicals published from roughly 1980 to the present.

Legal periodicals (not just the indexes) are available electronically in many law libraries through a subscription service called HeinOnline. Libraries can subscribe to the service and place it on their networks for patrons' use. HeinOnline allows searching for articles by keyword, author, title, and citation; it also allows a legal researcher to search the bodies of articles and to browse the table of contents of the periodicals. Many libraries choose to subscribe to HeinOnline because it provides access to periodicals published prior to 1980, unlike the print indexes, electronic indexes, and pay research databases. Thus, check with the office library or the nearest law library to see if it subscribes to this service.

Legal periodicals are available on LexisNexis and Westlaw also. One approach is to enter the citation of the article, if it is known, into the "Get a Document" feature on LexisNexis or the "Find by citation" feature on Westlaw. Another approach is to enter the general legal periodical database (see Table 2-3) or a particular periodical's database

---

2. An advisory group of the American Association of Law Libraries aids in the selection of periodicals for inclusion in *LegalTrac*.

Table 2-4. Electronic Media for Arizona Legal Periodicals

Arizona Legal Periodical	LexisNexis Database	Westlaw Database	Availability on Internet
Arizona Attorney	Bar Journals, Combined	JLR or TP-ALL	www.myazbar.org/AZAttorney
Arizona State Law Journal	Arizona Law Reviews, Combined	AZ-JLR	www.law.asu.edu/?id=529 (table of contents only)
University of Arizona Law Review	Arizona Law Reviews, Combined	AZ-JLR	www.law.arizona.edu/Journals/ALR/archive.htm (2000–present available)

and perform a word search. Neither LexisNexis nor Westlaw provides complete coverage for the legal periodicals available in their databases. Generally, these databases only carry the content of legal periodicals from 1980 to the present.

Some legal periodicals are available on free Internet sources. A quick search may be fruitful in order to find if a title provides its content on the Internet. At the very least, the Internet may provide the title's table of contents. Table 2-4 shows the availability of important Arizona legal periodicals in both pay research databases and free Internet sources.

VI. *American Law Reports*

American Law Reports (A.L.R.) provides a collection of case summaries on a specific legal topic.[3] Each collection of case summaries is known as an *Annotation*. Generally, an Annotation on a legal topic contains case summaries from all jurisdictions, both state and federal; thus, it provides a very thorough, detailed list of primary authority. An

---

3. *A.L.R.* volumes also reprint selected court decisions on each topic, but most researchers use only the case summaries because cases are reported in many other print and online resources.

Table 2-5. Outline of the Research Process in a Print-Media *A.L.R.*

Step 1: Generate research terms and use them to look in the *A.L.R.* index to locate a relevant Annotation.

Step 2: Find the *A.L.R.* volume containing the Annotation and read it.

Step 3: Review any pocket part for additional, relevant information.

Annotation does not analyze the cases, though. As such, using *A.L.R.* is a good first step in conducting research on a narrow legal issue.

Currently, there are six series of *A.L.R.* covering state law topics[4] (*A.L.R, A.L.R.2d, A.L.R.3d, A.L.R.4th, A.L.R.5th,* and *A.L.R.6th*) and two series of *A.L.R.* covering federal law topics (*A.L.R. Fed.* and *A.L.R. Fed. 2d*). Using *A.L.R.* in print media is a three-step process, as outlined in Table 2-5.

First, use a list of research terms in the index to locate the proper legal topic. The index to *A.L.R.* is located at the end of the set; this index is periodically updated by pocket parts in the back of the volumes. Once a relevant citation to an Annotation is located, locate the Annotation by finding the volume in which that Annotation is published and read the Annotation. Finally, review the back of the volume to see if there is a pocket part or supplement adding new information to the Annotation. Also check the list of superseded Annotations to see whether an Annotation has been replaced.

A.L.R. Annotations are also available in LexisNexis in the "American Law Reports and American Jurisprudence 2d, Combined" database and on Westlaw in the "ALR" database. When beginning research with the citation of an Annotation, enter the citation into the "Get a Document" feature on LexisNexis or the "Find by citation" feature on Westlaw. Without a specific citation, enter the *A.L.R.* database and perform a word search.

---

4. The Annotations in these *A.L.R.* volumes include summaries of federal law within the topic, if federal law applies.

**Table 2-6. Outline of the Research Process
in a Print-Media *Restatement of Law***

Step 1: Generate research terms and use them to look in the *Restatement of Law* subject index or table of contents to locate a relevant section.

Step 2: Find and read the *Restatement of Law* volume containing the relevant section and its comments.

Step 3: Review any Appendix volumes for references to cases interpreting or addressing the relevant section.

VII. *Restatements of Law*

The American Law Institute publishes a series of statements that summarize the most widely accepted common law in a specific area of law; they may also provide summaries on emerging areas of law. These summaries are generally known as *Restatements of Law*. *Restatements of Law* are available for the following subjects: agency, conflicts of law, contracts, foreign relations law of the United States, judgments, laws governing lawyers, property, restitution, security, suretyship and guaranty, torts, trusts, and unfair competition. The American Law Institute members are distinguished practicing lawyers, judges, and scholars. These members deliberate over various legal subjects and, according to the American Law Institute's website, publish the *Restatements of Law*, with the goals "to promote the clarification and simplification of the law and its better adaptation to social needs, to secure the better administration of justice, and to encourage and carry on scholarly and scientific legal work."[5] As such, some jurisdictions give persuasive weight to *Restatements of Law*, and sometimes courts will adopt them in the absence of mandatory authority.

Table 2-6 contains the steps for research *Restatements of Law* in print media. First, either search the subject index or browse the table

---

5. The American Law Institute's website is www.ali.org.

of contents for each volume. The subject listings and table of contents will refer to a specific section. Second, locate the relevant section in the volumes and read the section. It is also important to read the comments following the section. These comments provide examples of how the section applies to certain factual situations. Finally, check the Appendix volumes for references to relevant cases. The Appendix volumes are organized numerically by each section number. After locating the relevant section number in the Appendix volumes, read the case summaries from all jurisdictions that interpret or address this section. Remember to check for any pocket parts updating the current Appendix volume and to note that the Appendix volumes are not cumulative. Each volume in the Appendix covers a different period of time, so many volumes may have to be consulted to find all cases interpreting or addressing the section.

Restatements of Law are also available on pay research databases. They are located in the "Restatement Rules and Annotated Case Citations" database on LexisNexis and in the "REST" database on Westlaw.[6] Search for a *Restatement of Law* section by (1) entering the citation of an section, if it is known, into the "Get a Document" feature on LexisNexis or into the "Find by citation" feature on Westlaw, or (2) by entering a *Restatement of Law* database and performing a word search, as explained in Chapter 1.

---

6. Westlaw also has a separate database for each individual *Restatement of Law*. The list of these databases is available on the "REST" database search screen and in the Westlaw database directory.

Chapter 3

Researching Constitutions

Because a constitution defines the limits on a government's power, it is important to look for a relevant constitutional provision early in the research process. Specifically,

> The United States Constitution is the preeminent source of law in our legal system, and all other rules, whether promulgated by the state or the federal government, must comply with its requirements. Each state also has its own constitution. A state's constitution may grant greater rights than those secured by the federal constitution, but because a state constitution is subordinate to the federal constitution, it cannot provide lesser rights than the federal constitution does.[1]

I. Arizona Constitution

The Arizona Constitutional Convention adopted the Arizona Constitution on December 9, 1910, and the Arizona citizens ratified it on February 9, 1911. Due to an unusual requirement of the Enabling Act, the United States Congress and the United States President also needed to approve the Arizona Constitution. Although the United States Congress gave its approval, President Taft vetoed this approval due to a provision in the Arizona Constitution that allowed Arizona citizens to recall public officials, including judges. Congress then passed a resolution, which President Taft approved, that allowed Ari-

---

1. Amy Sloan, *Basic Legal Research: Tools and Strategies* 2 (3d ed., Aspen 2006).

zona to gain statehood if the Arizona citizens voted for an amendment removing judges from the recall provision. This vote happened on December 12, 1911, and Arizona officially became the 48th state. Interestingly, the Arizona citizens eventually restored the ability to recall judges in Article 8.[2]

The Arizona Constitution currently contains 28 articles, as detailed in Table 3-1. These articles are numbered from 1 to 29, with the addition of Article 6.1. Articles 23 and 24 dealt with prohibition and were repealed in 1932. The constitutional articles are divided into sections. For example, Article 9, Section 9 addresses the requirement that tax laws must be specific in their subject and object. Appendix 3-1 at the end of the chapter shows a sample Arizona Constitution section.

The Arizona Constitution is available in print media in *Arizona Revised Statutes Annotated*. The advantage of researching the Arizona Constitution in print media is that the constitution is *annotated*, which means that it contains extra research features. These features include historical notes as well as citations to relevant attorney general opinions, West digest key numbers,[3] treatises, forms, and secondary sources. These annotations also provide relevant cross-references to other laws, including the United States Constitution. Most importantly, the print media version of the Arizona Constitution contains Notes of Decisions for each constitutional provision. Notes of Decisions contain citations and summaries of cases that address or interpret the point of law in the constitution. To research the Arizona Constitution in print media, either (1) browse the relevant articles or (2) look in the index to *Arizona Revised Statutes Annotated* to find references to relevant constitutional articles and sections.

The Arizona Constitution is also available in electronic media. It is available for no cost on the Arizona State Legislature's website at

---

2. More detailed information on the Arizona Constitution's history is available at www.azsos.gov/public_services/Constitution/Constitution.pdf.

3. The West digest system is covered in Chapter 7.

Table 3-1. Arizona Constitution's Articles

1. State Boundaries
2. Declaration of Rights
3. Distribution of Powers
4. Legislative Department
5. Executive Department
6. Judicial Department
6.1 Commission on Judicial Conduct
7. Suffrage and Elections
8. Removal from Office
9. Public Debt, Revenue, and Taxation
10. State and School Lands
11. Education
12. Counties
13. Municipal Corporations
14. Corporations Other than Municipal
15. The Corporation Commission
16. Militia
17. Water Rights
18. Labor
19. Mines
20. Ordinance
21. Mode of Amending
22. Schedule and Miscellaneous
25. Right to Work
26. Right of Licensed Real Estate Brokers and Salesmen to Prepare Instruments Incident to Property Transactions
27. Regulation of Public Health, Safety, and Welfare
28. English as the Official Language
29. Public Retirement Systems

www.azleg.state.az.us/Constitution.asp.[4] The constitution on this website is searchable by words or phrases, but the website does not contain annotations.

Both LexisNexis and Westlaw provide the Arizona Constitution. Although these are pay research databases, they do offer the ability to search an annotated version of the constitution. The Arizona Constitution is available on LexisNexis in the "Arizona Revised Statutes, Constitution, Court Rules & ALS combined" database and on Westlaw in the "AZ-ST-ANN" database.

To search the Arizona Constitution on LexisNexis or Westlaw, either (1) search the table of contents for the Arizona Constitution or (2) perform a word search in a relevant database. To perform a table of contents search in LexisNexis, enter the constitution's database and use the constitution's table of contents under the search box. In Westlaw, first enter the constitution's database and then click on the tab for "Table of Contents" at the top of the search page. In either pay research database, clicking on an article in the table of contents allows a user to "drill down" with subsequent clicks to see the sections and subsections under each article. If there are no further sections or subsections, then clicking on any of the articles or sections will link directly to the first page of that article or section.

II. United States Constitution

Like the Arizona Constitution, the United States Constitution is available in both print and electronic media. The United States Constitution is published with annotations in *Arizona Revised Statutes Annotated*, *United States Code Annotated*, and *United States Code Service*; these volumes are explained in Chapter 4. To research the United States Constitution, either (1) browse the relevant articles and

---

4. The Arizona Constitution is also available on the Arizona Secretary of State's website at www.azsos.gov/public_services/Constitution/Constitution.pdf. This version of the constitution is not searchable and does not contain annotations.

amendments or (2) look in the index to the constitution to find references to relevant articles and amendments.

The United States Constitution is widely available at no cost in electronic media. Relevant websites and addresses include the following:

- Arizona Secretary of State
  www.azsos.gov/public_services/Constitution/Constitution.pdf
- Cornell University
  www.law.cornell.edu/constitution/constitution.overview.html
- National Archives
  www.archives.gov/national-archives-experience/charters/constitution.html
- Emory University
  www.law.emory.edu/cms/site/index.php?id=3080.

Although the Emory University website provides a search function, none of these websites contain annotations.

The United States Constitution is available on both LexisNexis and Westlaw. One LexisNexis database is "USCS - United States Code Service: Code, Const, Rules, Conventions & Public Laws." The Constitution is included in the Westlaw database "USCA." Both databases provide annotations. Either database can be searched through the table of contents for the United States Constitution or through a word search in a relevant database. The steps for performing these searches are the same as those for the Arizona Constitution explained in Section I above.

Appendix 3-1. Sample Arizona Constitution Article

Art. 9 § 9

§ 9. Statement of tax and objects

Section 9. Every law which imposes, continues, or revives a tax shall distinctly state the tax and the objects for which it shall be applied; and it shall not be sufficient to refer to any other law to fix such tax or object.

Cross References

Statement of object of tax and application of funds to object, see Const. Art. 9, § 3.

Library References

Statutes 121(1), 245.
WESTLAW Topic No. 361.
C.J.S. Statutes §§ 234, 376, 385.

Notes of Decisions

Construction and application 1

---

1. Construction and application

Requirement of this section that tax law state the tax sought to be collected and object for which proceeds shall be applied does not cover excise taxes. City of Glendale v. Betty (1935) 45 Ariz. 327, 43 P.2d 206; Gila Meat Co. v. State (1929) 35 Ariz. 194, 275 P. 1; Hunt v. Callaghan (1927) 32 Ariz. 235, 257 P. 648.

Ordinance ordering street improvement work did not impose tax within meaning of this section, and proposed assessment was not such tax. Collins v. City of Phoenix (C.C.A. 1931) 54 F.2d 770.

Amount required of applicant seeking to appropriate waters for irrigation and development of electrical energy, as a conditions precedent to filing and recording of permit applied for, was extracted from applicant as a "fee" and not as a "tax," and hence, this section relating to taxes would not be applicable. Steward v. Verde River Irrigation & Power Dist. (1937) 49 Ariz. 531, 68 P.2d 329.

Declaration of legislature as to nature of tax imposed will be given some effect by court in determining whether tax is a property tax or an excise tax, although such declarations are not conclusive. Stults Eagle Drug Co. v. Luke (1936) 48 Ariz. 467, 62 P.2d 1126.

This section, requiring that tax laws shall distinctly state object of tax, is mandatory. Tillotson v. Frohmiller (1928) 34 Ariz. 394, 271 P. 867.

Gasoline and mill taxes were not within this section, requiring law imposing tax to state tax and object. Hunt v. Callaghan (1927) 32 Ariz. 235, 257 P. 648.

Reprinted with permission of West, a Thomson business.

Chapter 4

Researching Statutes and Court Rules

After looking for any applicable constitutional provisions, next look for any relevant statutes. If a statute exists,[1] any court in that statute's jurisdiction is bound by the statute, although the court may interpret the statute's terms or may rule on the statute's constitutionality.

I. Print Media

Arizona, like most states and the federal government, has both an official and an unofficial statutory compilation; a statutory compilation is also known as a code in some jurisdictions. An *official code* is one that that a government or its designee publishes. In most states, including Arizona, the actual work of publishing the official state code is done by a third party and not by the state itself. Thomson West ("West") is Arizona's designated publisher for its official code.

An *unofficial code* is one that a commercial company publishes. Importantly, the text of a statute is available in either an official or unofficial code for the relevant jurisdiction, and there is no precedential difference between a statute published in an official code and a statute published in an unofficial code. If there is a conflict between the two types of codes, however, the official code governs. The dif-

---

1. The scope of this chapter is Arizona's state statutes. Many Arizona counties and cities have their own set of controlling rules. These rules can be found (1) on the relevant county or city website or (2) on the shelves in many Arizona libraries.

ference between a statute published in Arizona's official code and a statute published in an unofficial code is the set of extra features included in the code.

A. Arizona Print Media

Arizona Revised Statutes Annotated, commonly known as *A.R.S.*,[2] is the official code for Arizona and has been since 1956. *A.R.S.* is an *annotated code*, which means that it contains extra research features for each statute.[3] Most importantly, *A.R.S.* contains Notes of Decisions for each statute. Notes of Decisions contain summaries of cases that address or interpret the point of law in the statute, along with citations to those cases. *A.R.S.* annotations also contain notes on the statute's history, which is needed for legislative history research. Other helpful annotations include citations to relevant attorney general opinions; West digest key numbers;[4] treatises; forms; secondary sources; and cross-references to *Arizona Administrative Code*, *United States Code*, and other relevant laws, including uniform laws. Appendix 4-1 at the end of the chapter shows a sample Arizona statute with annotations.

A.R.S. contains other potentially useful features. These features include: (1) an annotated Rules of Court (see Section III below), (2) the Arizona Constitution, (3) the United States Constitution, (4) the Declaration of Independence, and (5) the Enabling Act and Election Ordinance of 1910 that gave the people of the Territory of Arizona the power to form a constitution and a state government.

A.R.S. is organized by subject and divided into 49 titles representing these subjects. The titles are then further divided into chapters, articles, and sections. Chapters and articles are organizational headings, and the section number refers to a statute. Arizona statutes are

---

2. *A.R.S.* is the abbreviation used by Arizona practitioners, although this differs from the official citation format for *Arizona Revised Statutes Annotated*. Citation formats are explained in Appendix A.

3. Many states have official codes that are not annotated. In these states, a legal researcher generally relies on the unofficial code for research, since it contains extra features, such as Notes of Decisions.

4. The West digest system is covered in Chapter 7.

located by both title number and section number. For example, the citation to Ariz. Rev. Stat. Ann. § 13-2306 means the statute is located in Title 13 under Section 2306.[5]

Table 4-1 shows the *A.R.S.* titles. *A.R.S.* is updated once per year with a pocket part in the back of each bound volume.

Table 4-1. *A.R.S.* Titles

Title 1 General Provisions

Title 2 Aeronautics (Repealed)

Title 3 Agriculture

Title 4 Alcoholic Beverages

Title 5 Amusements and Sports

Title 6 Banks and Financial Institutions

Title 7 Bonds

Title 8 Children

Title 9 Cities and Towns

Title 10 Corporations and Associations

Title 11 Counties

Title 12 Courts and Civil Proceedings

Title 13 Criminal Code

Title 14 Trusts, Estates and Protective Proceedings

Title 15 Education

Title 16 Elections and Electors

Title 17 Game and Fish

Title 18 Highways and Bridges (Repealed)

Title 19 Initiative, Referendum and Recall

Title 20 Insurance

Title 21 Juries

Title 22 Justices of the Peace and Other Courts Not of Record

Title 23 Labor

Title 24 Livestock and Animals (Repealed)

---

5. Appendix A explains legal citation more fully.

Table 4-1. *A.R.S.* Titles, cont'd.

Title 25 Marital and Domestic Relations

Title 26 Military Affairs and Emergency Management

Title 27 Minerals, Oil and Gas

Title 28 Transportation

Title 29 Partnership

Title 30 Power

Title 31 Prisons and Prisoners

Title 32 Professions and Occupations

Title 33 Property

Title 34 Public Buildings and Improvements

Title 35 Public Finances

Title 36 Public Health and Safety

Title 37 Public Lands

Title 38 Public Officers and Employees

Title 39 Public Records, Printing and Notices

Title 40 Public Utilities and Carriers

Title 41 State Government

Title 42 Taxation

Title 43 Taxation of Income

Title 44 Trade and Commerce

Title 45 Waters

Title 46 Welfare

Title 47 Uniform Commercial Code

Title 48 Special Taxing Districts

Title 49 The Environment

Since 2004, Lexis has published *Arizona Annotated Revised Statutes*, which is Arizona's unofficial code. Lexis republishes this code annually with updates. This unofficial code is numbered the same as *A.R.S.*, and it contains Notes of Decisions for all Arizona state cases since 1983 and all federal cases since 1991. It does not include the full panoply of extra features that are available in *A.R.S.* For this reason, most legal researchers rely on *A.R.S.* for researching Arizona's statutes, and the rest of this chapter will refer only to the features in *A.R.S.*

B. Federal Print Media

The official code for federal statutes is *United States Code (U.S.C.)*. It is an *unannotated code*, containing only the text of the federal statutes; it does not include any extra research features, such as references to cases or secondary sources. Thus, *United States Code* has limited research value.

The two unofficial codes for federal statutes are *United States Code Annotated (U.S.C.A.)* and *United States Code Service (U.S.C.S.)*. Both of these codes are annotated with helpful research features. *U.S.C.A.* is published by West, so its annotations are similar to those of *A.R.S.* Specifically, *U.S.C.A.* contains notes on each statute's history and cross references to related code provisions, as well as the other annotations explained above for *A.R.S.* Similar to *A.R.S.*, *U.S.C.A.* also contains Notes of Decisions for each statute.

As for *U.S.C.S.*, it contains the same extra research features that *U.S.C.A.* contains with one exception: *U.S.C.S.* does not include reference to West digest key numbers, since it is not published by West. *U.S.C.S.* does, however, contain comprehensive references to administrative agency regulations and actions.

Federal statutes are divided into 50 titles representing broad subjects. The titles are further sub-divided into chapters and sections. Similar to *A.R.S.*, to locate a federal statute, it is necessary to know both the title number and section number of the statute. The citation format is different from *A.R.S.*: 28 U.S.C. § 1332 is the statute in Title 28 (concerning the judiciary) that addresses federal question jurisdiction.

The text of the statute is the same in *U.S.C.*, *U.S.C.A.*, and *U.S.C.S.*, although *U.S.C.* is often out of date. The most current text is most likely to appear in *U.S.C.A.* or *U.S.C.S.*

C. Researching Print Media

The preliminary step in researching a statute is to figure out which jurisdiction to research. Each state government has its own code, and the federal government has its own code. After determining which

Table 4-2.
Outline of the Research Process for Statutes in Print Media

Step 1: Find the relevant statute(s) by using a finding feature.

Step 2: Read the statute(s).

Step 3: Read relevant cases interpreting the statute(s).

Step 4: Update the statute(s).

---

code to research, follow the outline for statutory research in Table 4-2. Although the following discussion explains how to research *A.R.S.*, this general discussion is applicable to researching any jurisdiction's annotated code.

1. Find the Relevant Statute

How to find a statute in print media depends on how much information the researcher knows and what types of finding features are contained in the relevant code. Table 4-3 shows the various types of finding features generally included in codes and when and how to use them. Each method is explained in more detail below. In each method, be sure to check the pocket parts for the most current information. A pocket part is a soft-bound pamphlet that is published more frequently than the hard-bound volumes of the code.

a. Starting with a Citation

With a current citation, finding a code section is as simple as locating the volume containing the correct title and flipping through that volume to find the section number.

b. Using the Conversion Table

If the researcher begins with a statutory citation that has changed because the statutes have been renumbered, or if the researcher knows the session law number for a statute, a conversion table is used. Look

Table 4-3. Finding Features for Statutes in Print Media

Finding Feature	When to Use the Feature	How to Use the Feature
Conversion Table	Used either (1) when the researcher has a statutory citation that has since changed because the statutes were renumbered or (2) when the legal researcher knows the session law number.	Look up the outdated statutory citation or session law number in the table and make note of the current statutory citations.
Popular Names Table	Used when the researcher knows the common name of the relevant statute(s) (e.g., "Clean Air Act").	Look up the name in the table and make note of relevant statutory citations.
Title Outline	Used to browse statutes that are classified and codified together (e.g., to find related statutes).	Start with a known statute and browse the nearby titles and chapters, or simply browse all titles and chapters.
Topical Index	Used when the researcher needs to find all statutes in a particular legal subject (e.g., "environmental") or when the legal researcher knows under what subject the statute is classified.	Look up the research terms in the index for relevant matches. Make note of potentially relevant statutory citations.

up the old statutory citation or the session law number, and note the current statutory citations.

c. Beginning with a Popular Name

Some statutes are known by their popular names, such as the "Clean Air Act" or the "Americans with Disabilities Act." Most statutory codes contain a popular names table; next to the name of the statute is the relevant statutory citation.

d. Scanning the Title Outline

Sometimes a legal researcher will be interested in browsing statutes that are classified and codified together. This research will be especially important when the researcher needs to find relevant definitions for a code section that contains undefined terms. It may also be important when looking for related statutes that may affect another statute known to be relevant to the project. Go to the relevant statute, and browse nearby sections. Or, turn to the outline for the title containing that particular section, and scan the title outline. Look for chapters or sections that seem relevant to the current project.

Another approach is to begin the research project by simply browsing all of the titles in the code. After locating a relevant title, scan its outline for chapters that may be on point. Then scan the sections under those chapters.

e. Using the Topical Index

Often statutory research begins with the researcher not knowing a relevant citation or popular name. In these instances, the researcher generates a list of research terms (refer to Chapter 1 for suggestions on developing helpful research terms). A thesaurus or legal dictionary may help while brainstorming research terms. Look in each code's topical index, which usually appears in soft-bound volumes at the end of the statutory series. Make note of potentially relevant statutory citations.

Remember that more than one statute may be relevant to an issue. In an index, the words "*et seq.*" following a statutory citation tell you to look at that statute, as well as the immediately following statutes. Generally, a statute is one part of a larger piece of legislation or an act. Frequently, it is important to find and read the entire act in order to understand how its parts work together. In addition, a term in an index may contain a cross-reference to another term included in the index. Follow up on these leads to find all relevant statutes.

2. Read the Statute

For each statutory citation in the notes generated in the previous step, locate the relevant title number in the *A.R.S.* volumes and turn through the relevant volume to find the specific section referenced in the citation; this is the statute.

It is key to read the entire statute at this step in the research instead of skipping ahead to another step or beginning a new research task. Each word in a statute has legal importance. Thus, read the statute carefully and decide which words may need further explanation in order to apply the statute. Then look for definitions of these words in a definition section; most likely, this definition section will be located in a previous statute. The best way to look for definitions within a code is to browse the Title Outline or simply turn through the pages of the relevant volume. This step may also reveal any closely related, applicable statutes that may have been missed in the previous step.

3. Read the Relevant Cases

Rarely does the statutory language alone answer a research question. Courts frequently provide relevant interpretations and definitions of statutory language. Courts also provide guidance on how to apply a statute to a set of facts. Thus, the next step is to review Notes of Decisions following the statute to find relevant cases. Notes of Decisions are summaries of cases that address or interpret the point of law in the statute; each note concludes with a case citation. After reading the Notes of Decisions and recording relevant case citations, the next step is to find the cases and read them, as the summaries are not legal authority. Chapter 6 explains how to use a citation to find a case.

4. Update the Statute

The last step in researching a statute is to update it and make sure it is still in effect. This step is particularly important when using print media because the hardbound volumes of a code are not frequently updated and replaced in whole.

The first way to update a statute is to look in the back of the volume for a pocket part, which updates the information in the volume, including the statutes and the Notes of Decisions. Sometimes a pocket part may be too thick to fit comfortably inside the back cover of a volume, so check the shelf space immediately behind the volume for a stand-alone pocket part.[6] A pocket part is numbered and organized in a manner identical to the bound volume. If a statute is not included in a pocket part, the statute has no updates as of the date of the pocket part. Be careful: the absence of a statute in a pocket part does not mean that the statute is no longer in effect. Also note that a newer statute may appear only in the pocket part and not in the hardbound volume. Thus, it is always important to check the pocket part.

The next way to update the statute is through an updating service. An updating service will provide information on the validity of a statute by giving information on whether the statute has been amended or repealed. An updating service will also provide citations to cases interpreting and applying the statute. Chapter 10 explains how to use updating services.

II. Electronic Media

Codes are also available in electronic media. Some of these media are free of charge, such as free Internet sources, while others are pay research databases. Consult Chapter 1 in deciding how to use electronic media cost effectively.

A. Arizona Electronic Media

Arizona statutes are available electronically directly from the Arizona State Legislature at www.azleg.state.az.us/ArizonaRevised-Statutes.asp.[7] The statutes on the Arizona State Legislature's site are updated regularly. The date of the last update is listed at the top of the page of the website. In addition, the statutes on this website are

---

6. In some codes, including *U.S.C.*, this stand-alone pocket part is known as a supplement.

7. Many Arizona libraries' websites provide links to the Arizona State Legislature website.

searchable. Click directly on a title to find a list of chapters and statutes under that title. Clicking on the statute's title brings up the statute's text. Unfortunately, this website is of limited research value as the statutes on this site are unannotated.

To search an electronic annotated version of Arizona statutes, use a pay research database. LexisNexis and Westlaw provide a searchable library of each state's materials, including Arizona statutes. On LexisNexis, Arizona statutes are located in the "AZ - Arizona Revised Statutes" database.[8] On Westlaw, Arizona statutes are located in the "AZ-ST-ALL" (Arizona statutes) database.[9] As explained more fully in Chapter 1, it is cost effective to locate the smallest possible database when researching on pay research databases.

B. Federal Electronic Media

Federal statutes are available electronically directly from the federal government and other reputable sources on several websites:

- Government Printing Office
  www.gpoaccess.gov/uscode/index.html
- United States House of Representatives
  http://uscode.house.gov
- Cornell University
  www.law.cornell.edu/uscode.

These websites are updated regularly and searchable, but they are unannotated.

Annotated versions of federal statutes are available on pay research databases. To find annotated federal statutes on LexisNexis,

---

8. A larger database on LexisNexis contains statutes and other documents as well: "AZ - Arizona Revised Statutes, Constitution, Court Rules & ALS, Combined."

9. Arizona statutes are also located in the "ST-ANN-ALL" database (all state statutes), but it should be used only when a 50-state survey is needed because it is much more expensive to use.

search the "United States Code Service - Titles 1 through 50" database. To find annotated federal statutes on Westlaw, search the "USCA" database. One benefit of searching statutes on a pay research database is that the list of interpretive cases can be searched by a word search by using "FOCUS" (LexisNexis) or "Locate" (Westlaw), as explained in Chapter 1.

C. Researching Electronic Media

The steps to researching a statute in electronic media mirror the four steps in print media: (1) finding the statute, (2) reading the statute, (3) reading relevant cases, and (4) updating the statute.

A citation can be used to locate a statute. On a free Internet source, begin with the code's title list. Select the title shown in the citation. On a pay research database, use the "Get a Document" function (LexisNexis) or "Find by citation" function (Westlaw) to find the statute. Both the "Get a Document" and the "Find by citation" features ask for the statutory citation in order to locate the statute; both pay research databases offer publication lists that show the citation format used by that database.

Both LexisNexis and Westlaw provide links to Popular Name Tables for some statutory codes. A researcher beginning with the common name of an act would use one of those services. If neither the relevant statute citation nor the popular name is known, generate research terms and perform a word search, as explained in Chapter 1.

The next steps when researching in electronic media are identical to the steps in print media: read the statute and any relevant cases interpreting the statute. These steps are explained earlier in section I.C.

Finally, update the statute. One advantage to working in electronic media is that there are no pocket parts to check. It is still important to check the date of the website or database to ensure that the information there is current. The second part of updating is to make sure the statute is still good law; updating services are explained in Chapter 10.

III. Court Rules

Court rules are the instructions for doing anything in court, from filing a complaint to garnishing someone's wages. Common examples of court rules include the Federal Rules of Civil Procedure and the Federal Rules of Criminal Procedure. Each jurisdiction has its own court rules, each court level within a jurisdiction may have its own court rules, and each individual court may have its own governing local court rules. Thus, it is important to know the jurisdiction that is applicable to the legal research problem and to be aware of the multiple layers of rules that may need to be consulted.

Most court rules are published in the applicable jurisdiction's code. In Arizona, the Arizona Rules of Civil Procedure and the Arizona Rules of Criminal Procedure are published in *A.R.S.* Similarly, the Federal Rules of Civil Procedure and the Federal Rules of Criminal Procedure are published in both *U.S.C.A.* and *U.S.C.S.* Thus, follow the same research steps for statutes in order to locate these court rules.

For other court rules, including local court rules, it is best to go directly to the court's website to find them. In Arizona, the Arizona Supreme Court website at www.supreme.state.az.us/rules provides some links to these rules. The Ninth Circuit Federal Court Rules are located at www.ce9.uscourts.gov, and the Federal District Court for the District of Arizona's court rules are located at www.azd.uscourts.gov.

Appendix 4-1. Sample Arizona Statute with Annotations

§ 13-2306. Possession of altered property; classification

A.   A person who is a dealer in property and recklessly possesses property the permanent identifying features of which, including serial numbers or labels, have been removed or in any fashion altered is guilty of a class 6 felony.

B.   It is a defense to a prosecution under this section that a person has lawfully obtained a special serial number pursuant to § 28-2165 or lawfully possesses the usual indicia of ownership in addition to mere possession or has obtained the consent of the manufacturer of the property.

Added by Laws 1977, Ch. 142, § 82, eff. Oct. 1, 1978. Amended by Laws 1978, Ch. 201, § 153, eff. Oct. 1, 1978; Laws 1980, Ch. 229, § 24, eff. April 23, 1980; Laws 1997, Ch. 1, § 33, eff. Oct. 1, 1997.

History and Statutory Notes

Source:

Based on Model Theft and Fencing Act as proposed by G.   Blakely and M.   Goldsmith, Criminal Redistribution of Stolen Property: the Need for Law Reform, 74 Mich. L. Rev. 1511-1626 (1976).

The 1978 amendment substituted "recklessly" for "knowingly" in subsec. A.; and substituted "it is a defense to a prosecution under this section that" for "The provisions of this section shall not apply to", "has" for "who", and "obtained" for "obtains", and deleted "who" following "§ 28-320" in subsec. B.

The 1980 amendment deleted ", without the consent of the manufacturer of the property," preceding "is guilty of" in subsec. A.; and added "or has obtained the consent of the manufacturer of the property" to subsec. B.

The 1997 amendment by Ch. 1 made a change in statutory citation reference to conform to the reorganization of Title 28.

Reviser's Notes:

1978 Note. Pursuant to authority of § 41-1304.02, "; classification" was added to the heading of this section.

Law Review and Journal Commentaries

From the Mafia to milking cows: State RICO Act expansion. 41 Ariz. L. Rev. 1133 (1999).

Library References

Receiving Stolen Goods 4.
WESTLAW Topic No. 324.

C.J.S. Receiving or Transferring Stolen Goods and Related Offenses §§ 4, 6 to 7, 12, 15, to 16

Notes of Decisions

Burden of proof 2
Conviction 1

1. Conviction

Where defendant's simultaneous possession of nine articles of altered property without serial numbers was proscribed by a single statute, this section, he could be convicted of only one count of possession. State v. Reisig (App. Div. 2 1980) 128 Ariz. 60, 623 P.2d 849.

2. Burden of Proof

In prosecution for possession of altered property, state would not be required to prove that defendant was a dealer in the type of property which formed basis of charges or that he was in fact dealing with the specified items. State v. Reisig, (App. Div. 2 1980) 128 Ariz. 60, 623 P.2d 849.

Reprinted with permission of West, a Thomson business.

Chapter 5

Researching Legislative History

Researching statutes has many facets. In addition to researching an enacted statute, as explained in Chapter 4, it is possible (1) to research a statute that has not yet been enacted, which is commonly known as *bill tracking*, and (2) to research the history of an enacted statute, which is commonly known as *legislative history*. In order to understand the documents located when tracking a bill or researching legislative history, it is important first to understand how the Arizona legislature operates.

I. How the Arizona Legislature Operates[1]

The Arizona State Legislature is responsible for making the laws that govern the State of Arizona. It meets for a 100-day session each year beginning in January, although the governor may call for a special session at any time in order to consider a specific issue. The Arizona legislature is made up of 90 total members in two chambers: 30 are members of the Senate, and 60 are members of the House of Representatives.[2]

Any legislator may introduce and sponsor a bill. A bill can be introduced in either chamber. Once introduced, the bill is sent to a

---

1. For a more detailed explanation of the Arizona State Legislature, visit the legislature's website at www.azleg.gov.
2. Arizona has 30 legislative districts, each of which elects one senator and two representatives. All legislators serve two-year terms and are limited to four consecutive terms.

standing committee. Standing committees vary in each legislative session, but these committees usually are formed to deal with particular areas of the law. This standing committee may "kill" the bill by not scheduling it for public hearing, or the standing committee may hold a public hearing on the bill, during which testimony is taken and amendments are considered. After the hearing, a majority of the standing committee can vote in favor of the bill, sending the bill to the entire house, called the Committee of the Whole (COW). If there is no majority vote in the committee, then the bill either is reworked for another vote or dies in committee.

Once the bill reaches the COW, the bill is debated and voted upon. If approved by a majority of the COW, the bill is sent to the other chamber for a similar committee process. If the second chamber approves the bill by majority vote, the bill is sent to the governor for signature.

The second chamber, however, may wish to craft some new language for the bill. If this happens, the bill is sent to a conference committee made up of members from both chambers. The conference committee's job is to craft compromise language, which then must be approved by majority vote of both chambers before it is sent to the governor for signature.[3]

After a bill becomes a law, it is assigned a chapter number. The Legislative Council then codifies this chapter into the *Arizona Revised Statutes Annotated*, by assigning it a place among the titles and sections. Chapter 4 explains how to search these titles and sections for the enacted law.

A. Arizona Bill Tracking

Simply put, a legal researcher tracks bills to learn whether some proposed legislation is close to passage or rejection. The first step in tracking a bill is to find the bill number of the proposed legislation.

---

3. If the governor vetoes the bill instead of signing it into law, the Arizona Legislature can override the decision by a two-thirds vote.

Table 5-1. Sample Arizona Bill Tracking on ALIS

BILL STATUS OVERVIEW
SB1102
SPONSORS: GARCIA P AGUIRRE P RIOS P
TITLE: vulnerable adults; financial exploitation
SENATE FIRST READ: 01/11/07
SECOND READ: 01/16/07
COMMITTEES: ASSIGNED COMMITTEES ACTION
01/16/07   FIIR
01/16/07   RULES
FINAL DISPOSITION: Held in Committees

If the bill number is unknown, perform a text search of the pending bills, memorials, and resolutions on the Arizona Legislative Information System (ALIS). ALIS is Arizona's official site for the legislature and is located at www.azleg.gov.[4] Hovering the mouse over the link to "Bills" on the top of the ALIS homepage, then clicking on "Bill Info," brings up a page to perform a keyword search of the text of any bill, memorial, or resolution in a legislative session. Although only one legislative session may be searched at a time, it is possible to browse all the bills, memorials, and resolutions, as links to them are provided in numerical order.

After locating the relevant bill number and having pulled up that bill on ALIS, click on the "Show Bill Overview" link to get the bill's summary and status. Specifically, this page provides every action taken on the bill. For example, Table 5-1 contains the "Bill Status Overview" page of a bill on financial exploitation of vulnerable adults. This bill was introduced in the 2007 legislative session.

Many versions of a bill, memorial, or resolution may exist, as either the House or the Senate may pass relevant amendments that require the bill to be reprinted with the new language. In some instances, the new language will be printed separately. Thus, it is a good idea to review the "Bill Status Overview" to find the most recent, updated version of the legislation.

---

4. Both LexisNexis and Westlaw also contain databases of Arizona's pending legislation. These are pay research databases, however, and their use for bill tracking is not cost effective or time saving.

Table 5-2. Outline of the Research Process for Legislative History
and Preferred Media

Research Step	Preferred Media
Step 1: Locate the relevant statute's session law to note the original chapter and bill number.	Any print or online version of the statute that contains historical notes
Step 2: Review the bill's journey through the legislative process by looking at its "Bill Status Overview."	ALIS (1995–present) LexisNexis/Westlaw (1988–1995) Print media (older than 1988)*
Step 3: Research secondary sources for commentary on the bill and research case law for decisions on the bill.	LexisNexis/Westlaw

* Both the print media and the pay research databases also contain information from 1995–present, but they are not as cost effective or as easy to use as ALIS.

B. Arizona Legislative History

If a statute is unclear on its face and a legal researcher needs help interpreting the statute's text, the researcher will search that statute's legislative history to find persuasive evidence of the drafters' intent. As such, legislative history research most often begins with a specific, enacted statute in mind. Legislative history is searchable in both print and electronic media,[5] although most legal researchers use of mixture of both media. An outline of the research process, and the preferred media for the research, appears in Table 5-2.

1. Research Using Electronic Media

The first step in researching legislative history is to determine the year the relevant statute was enacted or amended, and the corresponding chapter number. This information can usually be found in

─────────────

5. Both LexisNexis and Westlaw also contain databases to research Arizona legislative history. These are pay research databases, however, and their use for a full legislative history may not be cost effective. It is important to note that both services provide direct links to legislative history, if a statute, case, or secondary source cites to legislative history. This can be a useful, time-saving shortcut.

the historical notes printed immediately after the statute in *Arizona Revised Statutes Annotated*. (Do not confuse this list of citations with the "History & Statutory Notes" annotations that follow.) For example, in the statute shown in the appendix to Chapter 4, concerning altered property, the historical note begins by giving the 1977 act, which was codified in this statute, § 13-2306. Subsequent changes were made in 1978, 1980, and 1997. For the 1997 changes, the chapter number is Chapter 1, § 33.

This historical information is also on the LexisNexis and Westlaw displays of the statute. ALIS does not provide historical notes after its statutes, however. Alternatively, consult the library volumes of *Arizona Sessions Laws* or search for session laws on ALIS at www.azleg.gov by clicking on "Session Laws" under the drop-down menu under the "Bills" tab. Searching for session laws on ALIS is somewhat limited because it allows a user to search only one legislative session at a time and because only the session laws from 1995 to date are available.[6] The one advantage of using ALIS for searching session laws is the ability to use a keyword search to search the text of all the session laws in a single legislative session.

When researching a statute enacted from 1988 to 1995, use LexisNexis or Westlaw. Both LexisNexis and Westlaw contain Arizona legislative history information from 1988 to the present. Historical information is on LexisNexis in the "AZ - Arizona Advance Legislative Service" database and on Westlaw in the "AZ-LEGIS-OLD" database. For the current legislative session, use the "AZ Bill Tracking Reports" database on LexisNexis and the "AZ-BILLTRK" database on Westlaw. The advantage of using these pay research databases is that they are searchable with a word search.[7] When researching a statute enacted prior to 1988, use print media, which is explained in Section I.B.2 below.

The second step in researching legislative history is to look up the original chapter and bill number and note what happened to that bill in its journey through the legislative process. This step is most easily

---

6. Once on the session laws page, to change the legislative session click on the "Change Session" tab at the top of the page.

7. Word searching is explained in Chapter 1.

done on ALIS by searching for the relevant bill, and once the bill is on the screen, by clicking on the link for "Show Bill Overview." This overview provides a list of the bill's activity, the bill's sponsors, the committees that considered the bill, and the date the governor signed the bill into law. The link for "Bill Versions" provides the text of the various versions of the bill, while the link for "Adopted Amendments" provides any amendment information and language. The link for "Bill Summary/Fact Sheets" provides the bill's purpose and background, as well as the summary of actions taken on the bill. Appendix 5-1 at the end of this chapter shows a sample "Bill Status Overview" page of bill introduced and passed into law in 2004.

To find any relevant committee minutes, first note the committees that considered the bill. This information is most easily found on the "Bill Status Overview" page. Clicking on a committee link on this page will lead directly to that committee's meetings list with links to its minutes. This information is available only for bills enacted from 1995 to date. To do this research for older bills, use the print media, LexisNexis, or Westlaw. Starting with 2007, the Arizona State Legislature provides streaming video of various hearings and committee meetings. The website is http://azleg.granicus.com/ViewPublisher.php?view_id=3.

The third and final step is to research whether anyone or any court has commented on the statute's legislative history. To do this, research secondary sources and case law using the statute's citation or popular name as the keyword in the search.[8]

2. Research Using Print Media

In order to research the history of a bill passed into law prior to 1995 in print media, use the *Journal of the House* and the *Journal of the Senate* for the year in which the relevant bill was introduced. The House and Senate *Journals* are annual publications of the activities taken by the Arizona State Legislature. Look up the bill number in the table called "History of House and Senate Bills" and copy the list of actions taken on the bill. This step must be taken in both journals.

---

8. These research steps are explained in Chapters 2, 6, and 7.

Also note the names and dates of committee work on the bill. Another place to check for relevant committee work is in the "Committees" portion of the House and Senate *Journals.* Check the journals from the year the bill was introduced to the year the bill was signed. Also check the journals about two years prior to the bill's introduction in case any early investigative committee performed some work. Looking at the "Committees" portion of the journals for the bill will indicate if the legislature appointed any special, interim, or study committee to issue a report about the bill. Although no documents are available in these journals, the House Clerk at (602) 542-5297 or the Secretary of the Senate at (602) 542-4236 may have minutes of these meetings and any copies of reports generated. It may also be worth the time to check the State Law Library's Legislative Study Committee Reports at www.lib.az.us/is/state/lsc/index.cfm.

C. Research at the State Capitol

It may be necessary to travel to the Arizona State Capitol to find documents not available on ALIS or on the library's shelves. Make sure to keep detailed notes of what is unavailable on ALIS or at the library, as these notes will be helpful during a visit the House Clerk or the Senate Resource Center. Both offices retain bill files that may have reports and committee minutes, although they do not retain actual transcripts. The Senate has the last three years of both committee meetings and floor debates on audio tape and CD, while the House has audio tapes of committee meetings and floor debates from 1991. CDs of the House committee tapes are available from 2002 to date.

II. How the Federal Legislature Works

Similar to Arizona's bill process, a bill may be introduced into the U.S. House of Representatives or the Senate. Once introduced, the bill is sent to a committee, or even sub-committees, for hearings and testimony. If the committee votes in favor of the bill by a majority vote, the committee then recommends the bill to the originating body—the House or the Senate. This recommendation is made in a committee report. At this point, the bill is debated in front of the full House or Senate and voted upon. If the House or Senate votes in favor of the bill, the bill is then sent over to the other chamber for the process to begin again. It is possible that the House and Senate will approve different versions of a bill. If this happens, the bill is sent to a conference committee to be reworded. The conference committee is made up of members from both the House and the Senate. Only when both the House and Senate vote in favor of a bill containing the same language does the bill go before the President for signature or veto.[9]

After a bill becomes a law, the bill is given a public law number. A *public law number* shows the session of Congress in which the law was passed and the numerical order in which the bill was enacted (e.g., Pub. L. No. 101-336). Public laws are published in booklets known as *slip laws*. Later, the slip laws, which are identified by public law number, are compiled for a Congressional session. These *session laws* are published in *United States Statutes at Large* and given a new citation according to the volume number and page number of the *United States Statutes at Large* where they are published (e.g., 104 Stat. 328). The text of the public law, slip law, and session law are the same and follow a chronological organization.

Eventually, the session law is codified and placed into *United States Code*, which is organized by subject matter. This means that a session law will be divided into pieces according to subjects, and these individual pieces will be placed in *United States Code* where they fit. At this point, the laws are searchable by subject, as explained in Chapter 4.

A. Federal Bill Tracking

The easiest way to track a federal statute is to use either the Library of Congress website at http://thomas.loc.gov or the Government

---

9. Congress can override the President's veto with a two-thirds vote in favor of the bill.

Printing Office website at www.access.gpo.gov. Both sites contain bill summaries, status reports, Congressional hearing information, and floor debates on bills, although the exact coverage differs. Consider checking both sites when tracking a federal bill. Although both LexisNexis and Westlaw have databases for tracking federal bills,[10] these databases are not preferred by legal researchers because they are not cost effective to use and because their coverage of archived bills is not as extensive as the Government Printing Office (archives back to 1985) or the Library of Congress (archives back to 1973).

When using print media for tracking a federal bill, the *Congressional Record* is a good place to start. The *Congressional Record* is the official record of the proceedings and debates of the United States Congress. It contains the text of the debates on all bills in both the House and Senate, but it does not contain the actual text of the bills. When Congress is in session, it publishes the *Congressional Record* daily in pamphlets. This daily *Congressional Record* has two separate sections for House and Senate bills, and it contains two indexes: one organized by specific bill number and one organized by subject. Neither the indexes in the individual volumes nor the semi-monthly, soft-bound indexes printed separately are cumulative. Thus, while Congress is in session, a legal researcher would have to check the index of every volume or every soft-bound index in order to find all references to a relevant bill or subject.

When the Congressional session is over, the daily *Congressional Record* volumes for that session are printed together in a permanent *Congressional Record* volume. This permanent volume has its own cumulative index published separately. In addition, this permanent volume has different page numbers from the daily volumes, as the daily volumes are numbered separately for the House and Senate sections. The permanent volume does not make this division, and numbers pages consecutively. Be careful when looking at the citation to the

---

10. The LexisNexis database for current federal bill tracking is "Congressional Bills and Bill Tracking - Current Congress," and the database for historical bill tracking is "Federal Bill Tracking - Combined Archive" (coverage back to 1989). For Westlaw, the databases are "US-BILLTRK" and "BILLTRK-OLD" (coverage back to 1991), respectively.

Congressional Record to see whether that citation refers to the daily *Congressional Record* or the permanent *Congressional Record.*

B. Federal Legislative History

Federal legislative history research typically begins with a specific, enacted statute's citation. Look up the statute in an annotated code to find the statute's session law number and public law number, which are needed to research federal legislative history. In researching federal legislative history, a legal researcher is looking for materials from Congressional committees, including reports, and the transcripts of any floor debates.

Federal legislative history can be researched in both print and electronic media. As noted in Section II.A above, floor debates are located in print media in the *Congressional Record*. Committee reports, and any exhibits to those reports, can be found in print media in *United States Code Congressional and Administrative News* (*U.S.C.A.N.N.*) or in *Congressional Information Service* (*C.I.S.*). Committee reports are more persuasive than either floor debates or any exhibits. Because not many researchers use these print media, it is best to consult with a research librarian if you need to use these volumes.

There is one type of print media that many researchers do use regularly, however, because another researcher has already completed the work. These are the reference books containing compiled legislative histories for selected federal statutes. The two reference books to check are *Sources of Complied Legislative Histories*[11] and *Federal Legislative Histories.*[12]

As for electronic media, federal legislative history is available both on free Internet sources, as explained in Section II.A above: the Library of Congress website at http://thomas.loc.gov and the Govern-

---

11. Nancy P. Johnson, *Sources of Compiled Legislative Histories: A Bibliography of Government Documents, Periodical Articles, and Books* (AALL 1979–).

12. Bernard D. Reams, Jr., *Federal Legislative Histories: An Annotated Bibliography and Index to Officially Published Sources* (Greenwood Press 1994).

ment Printing Office website at www.gpo.gov. The information used for bill tracking in the current Congress becomes the legislative history of enacted statutes.

LexisNexis and Westlaw also contain databases of federal bills, selected committee reports, and floor debates in the *Congressional Record*, as well as databases of compiled legislative histories. Like the print versions of compiled legislative histories, the compiled legislative histories on the pay research databases are for major federal statutes. To find the specific coverage of these databases, search the database directory under legislative history information; it may take several additional clicks to find the compiled legislative history listings. It is generally more cost effective to research federal legislative history using the free Internet sources and to use LexisNexis and Westlaw only when the statute may be one of those included in the compiled legislative histories because much of the work has already been done.

Appendix 5-1. Sample Arizona Legislative History on ALIS

BILL STATUS OVERVIEW

HB2177

SPONSORS: STRAUGHN   P LOPEZ L   P LOREDO   P
              AGUIRRE A   C BIGGS   C DOWNING C
              FARNSWORTH C GALLARDO C GRAY C   C
              JACKSON, JR   C LOPES   C MEZA   C

TITLE: homeowners' associations; meetings; records

HOUSE FIRST READ: 01/19/04

COMMITTEES: ASSIGNED COMMITTEES ACTION

Vote Detail	01/19/04	FMPR	01/29/04 (8-0-0-1-0)	DP
Vote Detail	01/19/04	CMA	02/09/04 (10-0-0-2-0)	DPA
Vote Detail	01/19/04	RULES	02/11/04 (11-0-0-1-0)	C&P

SECOND READ: 01/20/04

MAJORITY CAUCUS 02/11/04 Y

MINORITY CAUCUS: 02/11/04 Y

COW ACTION 1: DATE   ACTION AYES NAYS NV EXC
                02/12/04 DPA   0   0   0   0

AMENDMENTS
CMA passed

THIRD READ: DATE   AYES NAYS NV EXC EMER AMEND RFE 2/3 VOTE RESULT
Vote Detail   02/16/04 56   1   3   0   Y   PASSED

TRANSMIT TO SENATE: 02/16/04

SENATE FIRST READ: 02/17/04

SECOND READ: 03/01/04

COMMITTEES: ASSIGNED COMMITTEES ACTION

Vote Detail	03/01/04	GOV	03/09/04 (9-0-0-0)	DP
	03/01/04	RULES	03/22/04	PFCA

MAJORITY CAUCUS: 03/23/04 Y

MINORITY CAUCUS: 03/23/04 Y

COW ACTION 1: DATE   ACTION AYES NAYS NV EXC
                03/31/04 DPA   0   0   0   0

AMENDMENTS
Amended by RULES - adopted

THIRD READ: DATE   AYES NAYS NV EXC EMER AMEND RFE 2/3 VOTE RESULT
Vote Detail   04/01/04 28   0   2   0   Y   PASSED

TRANSMIT TO HOUSE: 04/01/04

MAJORITY CAUCUS: 04/07/04   Y

MINORITY CAUCUS: 04/07/04   Y

                    Concurrence recommended

HOUSE CONCURRENCE: DATE   AYES NAYS NV EXC
                04/13/04 0   0   0   0

HOUSE FINAL READ: DATE   AYES NAYS NV EXC EMER RFE 2/3 VOTE RESULT
Vote Detail   04/13/04 50   8   2   0   PASSED

TRANSMITTED TO: GOVERNOR   04/13/04

ACTION: SIGNED   04/19/04

CHAPTER: 114

CHAPTERED VERSION: Senate Engrossed Version

Chapter 6

Finding Cases in Reporters and Online

The word *case* is a shorthand label for a court's written opinion or decision. Each case explains a court's decision in a particular dispute. A court can decide whether to publish a case or not to publish a case; the choice often rests on the precedential value the court sees in the case. Generally, a published case is available in both print and electronic media, while an unpublished case is either available only in electronic media or from the court.[1] Although some courts allow attorneys to use and cite unpublished cases, these cases only have persuasive precedential value.

The key to locating a case is to use its citation.[2] Basically, a case's citation references the case's location in print, including the specific volume and page number of the book in which the case is published. For example, the citation for the case *Nielson v. Patterson* is 204 Ariz. 530, meaning it can be found in volume 204 of *Arizona Reports* on page 530. A case's citation remains the same even for electronically published versions of the case.[3] In addition, the text of the case is the same regardless of whether the case is accessed in print or electronic media. What differs among the various print and electronic versions

---

1. Some unpublished cases from the federal courts of appeals are available in print. They have been printed in *Federal Appendix* since 2001.

2. For an explanation of legal citation formats, see Appendix A.

3. Some cases, such as unpublished cases, are available only electronically. These cases have unique electronic citations, as explained in Appendix A.

of a case is the type and number of editorial enhancements (sometimes referred to as finding aids) the publishers add to the case.

I. Print Media

Cases available in print are organized in sets of books called reporters. A *reporter* is a book that contains cases from a jurisdiction (or several jurisdictions); the cases are organized chronologically and not by topic or subject matter. Thus, unless the specific case citation is known, a legal researcher will not be able to approach the shelves of reporters and locate the case. It is helpful to think of using a reporter like using the business white pages of a telephone book: the business white pages are an organized listing of phone numbers (cases), but unless the user knows the specific name of an auto mechanic (the citation), for example, the user will not be able to use the business white pages to locate an auto mechanic's phone number. Chapter 7 addresses how to research digests and online sources when beginning research without relevant case citations (similar to searching the yellow pages in the analogy above).

Reporters can be categorized into one of two general types: official or unofficial. An *official reporter* is one that a government or its designee publishes; an *unofficial reporter* is one that a commercial company publishes. The most common unofficial reporters are the regional reporters published by Thomson West ("West"). *Regional reporters* are reporters that include cases from several states. West divided the states among the regional reporters for ease of publishing. This division does not track the division of states into the circuit courts, though, and does not enhance the precedential value of cases that happen to be published in the same regional reporter. Table 6-1 indicates which state's cases are located within each regional reporter.

As Table 6-1 shows, West has published several series of each regional reporter. When a reporter is divided into series, this means that West decided to start renumbering the reporter volumes at a certain point. For example, when *Pacific Reporter* reached volume 300 in 1931, West numbered the next volume as Volume 1 of *Pacific Re-*

Table 6-1. Coverage of Regional Reporters

Reporter and Abbreviation	States Included in Regional Reporter
Atlantic Reporter (A, A.2d)	Connecticut, Delaware, District of Columbia, Maine, Maryland, New Hampshire, New Jersey, Pennsylvania, Rhode Island, Vermont
North Eastern Reporter (N.E., N.E.2d)	Illinois, Indiana, Massachusetts, New York, Ohio
North Western Reporter (N.W., N.W.2d)	Iowa, Michigan, Minnesota, Nebraska, North Dakota, South Dakota, Wisconsin
Pacific Reporter (P., P.2d, P.3d)	Alaska, Arizona, California, Colorado, Hawaii, Idaho, Kansas, Montana, Nevada, New Mexico, Oklahoma, Oregon, Utah, Washington, Wyoming
South Eastern Reporter (S.E., S.E.2d)	Georgia, North Carolina, South Carolina, Virginia, West Virginia
South Western Reporter (S.W., S.W.2d, S.W.3d)	Arkansas, Kentucky, Missouri, Tennessee, Texas
Southern Reporter (So., So. 2d, So. 3d)	Alabama, Florida, Louisiana, Mississippi

porter, Second Series. West then started *Pacific Reporter, Third Series* after the second series reached Volume 999 in 2000. Be careful to use the right reporter series when locating a case; remember that older cases are located in the lower-numbered series.

Generally, a legal researcher can find a case in both an official and unofficial reporter.[4] Arizona cases are found in *Arizona Reports* (official) and *Pacific Reporter* (unofficial). There is no precedential difference between a case published in an official reporter and a case published in an unofficial reporter; however, if there is a conflict between the two printed versions, the official reporter version controls. Also, some courts require that lawyers cite to the official reporter in documents filed with that court. Court rules generally dictate whether this

---

4. Some states, however, do not publish an official reporter.

is required. In Arizona, Arizona Rules of Civil Appellate Procedure Rule 13(a)(6) require citation to both the official reporter and the unofficial reporter for Arizona cases, if possible. The only difference between a case published in an official reporter and a case published in an unofficial reporter is the set of editorial enhancements.

A. Editorial Enhancements of an Arizona Case

Although the specific editorial enhancements that a publisher provides differ from publisher to publisher, there are some typical enhancements that are more common than others. These include the case citation(s), the case caption, the case dates, the case synopsis, and the headnotes. Editorial enhancements have no precedential value; they are intended to help a lawyer to read and understand the case. Cite to the body of the opinion as precedent.

For Arizona cases, the editorial enhancements in *Arizona Reports* and *Pacific Reporter* are identical because West publishes both reporters. Appendix 6-1 at the end of the chapter shows the first page of an Arizona case with its editorial enhancements.

The *case citations*, which appear in the page header and just above the case caption, indicate the case's parallel citations. A *parallel citation* is a citation to another reporter in which the case is also published. Any of these case citations can be used to locate the case, as the body of the court's opinion in each reporter is the same.

The *case caption* provides the parties' names and their roles in the litigation. In a trial court case, the party bringing the lawsuit is referred to as the *plaintiff*, and the defending party is referred to as the *defendant*. If the trial court case is appealed, the party bringing the appeal is referred to as the *appellant*, and the defending party is referred to as the *appellee*, regardless of their original roles in the trial court. If in turn the appellate court case is appealed to the highest court, the party bringing the appeal is referred to as the *petitioner*, and the defending party is referred to as the *respondent*.

The *docket number* is the case number assigned by the deciding court. If a legal researcher needs to find documents filed with the court, the researcher would use this docket number to locate those documents. Although the docket number formats vary among courts, an Arizona docket number generally begins with a two-letter abbreviation for the case type; the most common two-letter abbreviations are CR for criminal cases and CV for civil cases. These letters are followed by a two-to-four digit number indicating the year in which the case was filed and a four-to-six digit case number. The docket number may also contain the assigned judge's initials or an abbreviation of the court. For example, CA-CV 03-0199 was a civil case decided by the Court of Appeals in 2003.

The *court information* provides the full name of the court that decided the case. This information may also include the division or department of the court that decided the case.

The *case dates* indicate when important procedural events occurred in the case, such as when the court held the hearing and when the court decided the case. The most important of these dates is the date the case was decided; this information is included in the case citation, as discussed further in Appendix A.

The *synopsis* is a short summary of the case. It generally provides a summary of the case's facts, important procedural aspects, key reasoning, and the court's conclusion, also known as a *disposition*. In the excerpt from the *Magee* case shown in this chapter's appendix, the synopsis includes the background and the holding, as well as the disposition "affirmed." The synopsis plays an important role in the early stages of a legal research project, as its summary helps in the decision whether to read the case in depth.

Finally, the *headnotes* operate as a table of contents to the case. Each headnote is a short summary of an important legal principle discussed in the case. The headnotes are numbered, and these numbers correspond to numbers the publishers add to the body of the opinion at the point where each new legal principle is discussed.[5]

---

5. In cases published by West, these headnotes also contain references to relevant topics and key numbers, as explained in Chapter 7.

Because most cases discuss many legal principles, the headnotes operate as a table of contents, allowing a researcher to quickly locate a relevant legal discussion without having to read the entire case. Headnotes also help in locating other cases discussing the same legal principle. The process of using headnotes to locate and research other similar cases is explained in Chapter 7.

As stated above, the only part of a case that has precedential value and should be cited is the opinion. The opinion is usually preceded by the name of the attorneys representing the parties, the names of the judges who heard the case (which sometimes are listed at the end of the case, depending on the jurisdiction), and the name of the judge who wrote the opinion.[6] If not all judges agree on a case's outcome, there will be more than one opinion. The *majority opinion* is the opinion that more than half of the judges support. The *dissenting opinion* is written by the judge(s) who disagree(s) with the majority opinion; the dissenting opinion is not binding, but it may be used as persuasive authority. It is also possible that a judge agrees with the outcome of the majority opinion but for different reasons than those reasons cited in the majority opinion. If this is the case, that judge may write a *concurring opinion*; it too may be used as persuasive authority. Finally, if there is no majority of judges supporting an opinion, the opinion with the most support will decide the case. This deciding opinion is called a *plurality opinion*.

B. Arizona Print Media

Like most other state courts, Arizona does not publish its trial court opinions. Arizona does publish the Arizona Court of Appeals and the Arizona Supreme Court opinions. Table 6-2 shows the various locations of these opinions in the reporters.

---

6. The "J." in this section stands for "judge" in the trial and appeals courts and "justice" in the highest court of a jurisdiction. A "C." preceding the "J." stands for "chief." If no judge takes credit for authoring the opinion, the term "*per curiam*" will appear in place of the judge's name.

Table 6-2. Arizona Reporters

	Official Reporter	Unofficial Reporter
Arizona Supreme Court Cases	*Arizona Reports* (1866–present)	*Pacific Reporter* (1883–1931) —*Second Series* (1931–2000) —*Third Series* (2000–present)
Arizona Court of Appeals Cases	*Arizona Appeals Reports* (1965–1976) *Arizona Reports* (1976–present)	*Pacific Reporter* —*Second Series* (1965–2000) —*Third Series* (2000–present)

Similar to most states, Arizona makes its courts' published cases available prior to these cases' publication in reporters, since it takes several months to compile cases and publish a reporter volume. *Advance sheets* are soft-bound booklets that publish the text of cases before they are published in a reporter. Advance sheets are generally available a few weeks after a court decides a case. Specifically, *Arizona Advance Reports* are published every two weeks and include cases from both the Arizona Court of Appeals and the Arizona Supreme Court. *Arizona Advance Reports* also contains semi-annual case and subject indexes, a cumulative case name table, and a table of parallel citations to *Arizona Reports* and *Pacific Reporter*. In addition, slip opinions are another even faster way to receive Arizona cases soon after they are decided. A *slip opinion* is a court's own publication of a case. Slip opinions are generally available directly from the court within hours or days after the case is decided. To find a slip opinion, use the parties' names or the docket number to make a request at the clerk's office.

C. Federal Print Media

Federal cases are also published in reporters (see Table 6-3). Selected cases from the United States District Courts (the federal trial

Table 6-3. Federal Reporters

	Official Reporter	Unofficial Reporter
Supreme Court Cases	*United States Reports*	*Supreme Court Reporter* *United States Supreme Court Reports, Lawyers' Edition*
Court of Appeals Cases	none	*Federal Reporter* *— Second Series* *— Third Series*
District Court Cases	none	*Federal Supplement* *— Second Series*

courts) are available in *Federal Supplement* and *Federal Supplement, Second Series*. Cases from the United States Courts of Appeals (the federal intermediate appeals courts) are available in *Federal Reporter; Federal Reporter, Second Series;* and *Federal Reporter, Third Series.* Although these reporters are unofficial reporters, legal researchers use them extensively for locating federal case law, as these reporters are readily available and reliable. Since 2001, West has also published the United States Courts of Appeals' unpublished cases, or cases with no precedential value, in *Federal Appendix.*

Cases from the United States Supreme Court are available in three different reporters. The official reporter is *United States Reports.* Because it is the official reporter, cite to it if possible. This is not always possible because *United States Reports* is the slowest of the three reporters to publish new cases; it can take several years for a case to be published in *United States Reports.* West's *Supreme Court Reporter* is published faster and is the first choice of many researchers looking for recent U.S. Supreme Court cases. Finally, U.S. Supreme Court cases are also published in *United States Supreme Court Reports, Lawyers' Edition*, often referred to as simply *Lawyers' Edition.*

In addition to the federal reporters, there are other print sources for federal cases, such as topical reporters and news services. *Topical reporters* publish cases on a specific subject. For instance, *Federal Rules Decisions* publishes federal cases that analyze criminal and civil rules of procedure, while *Bankruptcy Reporter* publishes cases on bankruptcy. As for news services, the most well known is *United States Law Week*, which provides summaries of important federal and state cases and provides the full text of all cases from the U.S. Supreme Court.

II. Electronic Media

Cases are widely available online on both pay research databases and free Internet sources. The two major pay services are LexisNexis and Westlaw.[7] Typing a case citation into the "Get a Document" function on LexisNexis or the "Find by citation" function on Westlaw will bring up the case. Both pay research databases offer publication lists that show the citation format used by that database. Without a case citation, the best option is to search the LexisNexis or Westlaw databases to locate a case.[8] Searching is generally allowed by research terms, a party's name, a judge's name, or a date, among other options.

As for free Internet resources, be cautious in choosing to rely on these resources, even though they are cost-effective alternatives to the pay research databases. First, if a website is not administered by the state or federal government or its designee, it is possible the information on the website may be incorrect or incomplete. Second, some websites with legal information provide no way to search the information. Finally, some websites with legal information provide no way to update or verify the cases to ensure the cases are still good law.[9]

A good, free website to start with is FindLaw at www.findlaw.com, which contains links to both state and federal legal sources. Another option is to start with the deciding court's website. Many jurisdictions publish their cases within hours after they are decided. Many times

---

7. There is another pay research database that some legal researchers use called Loislaw. Information on this service can be found at www.loislaw.com.

8. These search techniques are explained in Chapter 7.

9. Updating is covered in Chapter 10.

these court websites are searchable by parties' names, dates, or docket numbers.

A. Arizona Internet Resources

Since 1998, the Arizona Court of Appeals and Arizona Supreme Court have made their slip opinions available online at www.supreme .state.az.us/opin. The opinions on this website are searchable.

Although Arizona trial court opinions and orders are not available online, many Arizona trial courts provide case histories and calendar information. For example, the Maricopa County Superior Court provides this information at www.superiorcourt.maricopa.gov/docket/ index.asp. These trial court opinions will look different from the Arizona cases published in the reporters because the trial court opinions will not have any editorial enhancements. Specifically, the court's opinion will begin directly after the case caption; there will be no synopsis or headnotes.

B. Federal Internet Resources

United States Supreme Court slip opinions are available within hours of their decision at www.supremecourtus.gov/opinions/ opinions.html. In addition, Cornell University's website at http:// supct.law.cornell.edu/federal/opinions.html provides access to the federal courts' slip opinions relatively quickly after the courts' decisions. The federal courts of appeals and federal district courts are also in the process of providing access to both published and unpublished cases directly on their websites. For example, Ninth Circuit Court of Appeals slip opinions are available at www.ca9.uscourts.gov/ca9/ newopinions.nsf, and Federal District Court for the District of Arizona slip opinions are available at www.azd.uscourts.gov/azd/ courtopinions.nsf.

Appendix 6-1. Editorial Enancements of an Arizona Case

206 Ariz. 589

In re the Marriage of Martha Hale MAGEE, Petitioner–Appellee,

v.

Peter MAGEE, Respondent–Appellant.

No. 1 CA–CV 03–0199.

Court of Appeals of Arizona,
Division 1, Department A.

Jan. 8, 2004.

Background: Husband and wife engaged in post-decree proceedings in dissolution action. The Superior Court, Maricopa County, Cause No. DR 99–001577, A. Craig Blakey, II, J., ordered husband to pay additional attorney fees incurred by wife. Husband appealed.

Holdings: The Court of Appeals, Sult, J., held that:

(1) attorney fees statute requires showing only of financial disparity between husband and wife, rather than one spouse's actual inability to pay fees, and

(2) additional award of fees was proper exercise of discretion in this case.

Affirmed.

1. Appeal and Error ⚖984(5)

Court of Appeals reviews an award of attorney fees to determine whether it constituted an abuse of discretion.

2. Divorce ⚖224

Statute allowing award of attorney fees in dissolution actions requires showing only of financial disparity between husband and wife, rather than one spouse's actual inability to pay fees; requiring payment of spouse's fees is derived and justified from duty to support, which is not conditioned on receiving spouse's being destitute. A.R.S. § 25–324.

3. Divorce ⚖224

Although one spouse's ability to pay attorney fees in a dissolution action does not disqualify that spouse from being awarded attorney fees, ability to pay is one factor the court may consider when exercising its discretionary function of determining whether an award of fees is appropriate. A.R.S. § 25–324.

4. Divorce ⚖224

Additional award of $25,000 in attorney fees to wife in post-dissolution-decree proceeding was proper exercise of discretion, where husband's financial resources were substantially greater than wife's, both parties had taken reasonable positions in proceeding, and nothing indicated that fee award was tool to equalize the division of property. A.R.S. § 25–324.

John Friedeman, P.C. By John Friedeman, Phoenix, Attorneys for Appellant.

Lynn M. Pearlstein, Ltd. By Lynn M. Pearlstein, Phoenix, Attorneys for Appellee.

OPINION

SULT, Judge.

¶ 1 Peter Magee, Husband, appeals from an order of the trial court requiring him to pay attorneys' fees incurred by his wife, Martha Magee, in post-decree proceedings in the parties' dissolution action. According to Husband, the award is not authorized under Arizona Revised Statutes ("A.R.S.") § 25–324 (2000) because Wife did not show that she was unable to pay her own fees, which Husband contends is the statutory predicate for consideration for an award. We disagree that A.R.S. § 25–324 requires a showing of actual inability to pay as a predicate for consideration, and we conclude that all a spouse need show is that a relative financial disparity in income and/or assets exists between the spouses. Because that disparity exists between these parties, the trial court properly found that Wife was eligible for consideration, and the court consequently

Chapter 7

Researching Cases in Digests and Online

Without the citation to a case, a legal researcher cannot go straight to the reporters and find the case in a volume or go straight to the retrieval function on LexisNexis or Westlaw and pull up the case on the computer screen. Thus, in many instances, a legal researcher begins research of cases by using West's digest system or the equivalent search function in electronic media.

A *digest* is a set of books that organizes case summaries by topic or subject, instead of chronologically. Basically, using a digest is like using the yellow pages in a telephone book: the entries are organized by topics and sub-topics. For example, to find an auto mechanic's name (a case citation), find the topic entry for "auto mechanic" and search the listings to find an auto mechanic who meets the search criteria. This type of subject searching for case citations is available in both print and electronic media.

I. Print Media

The most commonly available print digests are published by Thomson West ("West"). As it did with its reporters, West divides the states into regions for ease of publishing digests; this division tracks the division of states into the regional reporters. As it has done with the regional reporters, West has published several series of each regional digest, each series containing summaries of cases published in a specified span of years. Table 7-1 indicates which state's cases are

Table 7-1. Coverage of Regional Digests

Regional Digest	States Included in Regional Digest
Atlantic Digest	Connecticut, Delaware, District of Columbia, Maine, Maryland, New Hampshire, New Jersey, Pennsylvania, Rhode Island, Vermont
North Western Digest	Iowa, Michigan, Minnesota, Nebraska, North Dakota, South Dakota, Wisconsin
Pacific Digest	Alaska, Arizona, California, Colorado, Hawaii, Idaho, Kansas, Montana, Nevada, New Mexico, Oklahoma, Oregon, Utah, Washington, Wyoming
South Eastern Digest	Georgia, North Carolina, South Carolina, Virginia, West Virginia

located within each regional digest. Only those regional digests that are currently published are included in Table 7-1. West no longer publishes *North Eastern Digest*, *South Western Digest*, and *Southern Digest*.[1]

In addition to these regional digests, West publishes digests for many state reporters, including Arizona, and for federal reporters. Arizona case summaries are available in both *Arizona Digest* and *Pacific Digest*. The main difference between the two digests is that *Arizona Digest* includes case summaries of federal cases interpreting and applying Arizona law while *Pacific Digest* does not include any federal case summaries.

Federal case summaries are available in *Federal Practice Digest*. This digest includes citations to cases of the federal district courts (cases reported in *Federal Supplement*), the federal appellate courts (cases reported in *Federal Reporter*), and the U.S. Supreme Court. Case

---

1. To find cases from the jurisdictions that were included in *North Eastern Digest*, *South Western Digest*, and *Southern Digest*, use state-specific digests. Remember, however, that *North Eastern Reporter*, *South Western Reporter*, and *Southern Reporter* are still published, so cases can be found in those reporters once a relevant citation is located in a state-specific digest.

summaries for the U.S. Supreme Court are also digested in *United States Supreme Court Digest*.[2]

Some digests are cumulative, while others are not. Specifically, *Arizona Digest* is a cumulative digest, meaning that one set of books indexes all Arizona cases. *Federal Practice Digest* and *Pacific Digest* are not cumulative, however. *Federal Practice Digest, Fourth* covers cases from the mid-1980s to the present, and *Federal Practice Digest, Third* covers cases from 1975 to the mid-1980s. To find cases published before 1975, use an earlier digest series. Similarly, the currently published *Pacific Digest* covers cases from Volume 585 of *Pacific Reporter, Second Series* to the present. To find older cases, use earlier published versions of *Pacific Digest* or use a state-specific digest.

In order to facilitate researching all jurisdictions at once, West publishes *Decennial Digest*. This set of digests allows a legal researcher to conduct survey research because it contains the headnotes from all state and federal cases. As would be expected, this set of digests contains many non-cumulative volumes and is quite large and cumbersome to use.

A. Organization of the Digest System

West summarizes a case by writing a headnote about each legal point in the case. As explained in Chapter 6, a headnote appears at the beginning of a case, prior to the court's opinion. A case may contain many separate headnotes. West also assigns each headnote a topic and a key number, which are explained below. Once each headnote in a case has been written and assigned its topic and key number, West then copies each headnote (with its topic and key number) for reprint in the digest system. West reprints each headnote in the digest system along with the citation to the case from which it originated. Thus, to find a case citation, use the digest system to read the reprinted headnotes.

---

2. *United States Supreme Court Digest, Lawyers' Edition* is another available digest of U.S. Supreme Court cases. Although it contains references to headnotes, it is important to note that these headnotes do not follow the same format or organization as West's digest system.

1. Headnotes

A *headnote* is a short summary of an important legal principle discussed in a case.[3] The headnotes are printed in the order that their respective legal points appear in the case. Generally, a headnote is no more than a sentence or two, and these sentences may be taken directly from the case. Each headnote is also preceded by its assigned topic and key number. Despite their utility in research, headnotes are not legal authority and should never be cited as such.

2. Topics and Key Numbers

All West digests organize case headnotes by topics and key numbers. A *topic* is a broad subject heading assigned to a legal point in a case. West currently has more than 400 topics. An example of a topic is "Divorce." A *key number* is an actual number assigned to a subdivision of the broad topic. For example, the key number 224 refers to the sub-division "Allowance for Counsel Fees and Expenses-Grounds" under the topic " Divorce." Some topics, like "Criminal Law," contain more than 1,000 key numbers, while other topics contain fewer than twenty.

B. Research Using the Digest System

The four basic steps for finding case citations using the digest system are outlined in Table 7-2.

1. Determining the Correct Digest

First, determine which jurisdiction controls the research question and then choose a digest that includes that jurisdiction's headnotes. Although headnotes for a case may be printed in more than one digest (for example, Arizona headnotes are available in both *Arizona Di-*

---

3. The headnotes referred to in this chapter are West's headnotes. Other publishers and pay research databases, such as LexisNexis, have their own versions of headnotes, which do not match West's headnotes.

Table 7-2. Outline of the Research Process in a Print-Media Digest

Step 1: Determine the correct digest to use.

Step 2: Locate relevant topics and key numbers in the digest.

Step 3: Read the headnotes organized under the relevant topics and key numbers.

Step 4: Update the research.

gest and *Pacific Digest*), the topic, key numbers, and text of the headnotes remain the same. Thus, it is advantageous to choose the smallest digest—generally the digest that contains only one jurisdiction—in order to minimize the number of headnotes that must be read.

2. Locating Relevant Topics and Key Numbers

a. Beginning with a Relevant Case

In determining the relevant topic and key number for a legal point, it is advantageous to use any clues already found in the research. Specifically, after locating one case that is relevant to your research issue, use the topic and key number from any relevant headnote as a starting point. Turn directly to the digest volume that includes that topic and key number, and begin reading the headnotes to find citations to other cases. For example, to find other cases like the *Magee* case in the appendix to Chapter 6, which discusses grounds for awarding attorneys' fees in a divorce action, find the relevant topic and key number from the headnotes to the case: "Divorce 224." Then go to *Arizona Digest* and look under "Divorce 224" to find other Arizona cases that discuss grounds for awarding attorneys' fees in a divorce action. This same topic and key number can be used in any other West digest, such as *New Mexico Digest*, to find other cases that discuss the same issue. This is because topics and key numbers are the same in all West digests.

b. Beginning with a Topic

A legal researcher may already have some familiarity with a topic and know which digest volumes contain that topic. In this instance, the legal researcher can go directly to the digest volume and browse the overview of that topic to find relevant key numbers. An overview of each topic's sub-divisions is located at the beginning of each topic.

c. Beginning with the Descriptive Word Index

When you do not know where to begin a research project, use the Descriptive Word Index. The Descriptive Word Index is a several-volume index organized by subjects; it is generally located at the beginning or end of a digest set. Use the Descriptive Word Index by looking up research terms; entries in the index will contain references to their respective topics and key numbers. Take notes of any on-point topics and key numbers. Because the Descriptive Word Index is a hardbound index that is updated by pocket parts between printings, check the pocket parts to make sure all new material has been considered.

After generating a list of potentially helpful topics and key numbers, a legal researcher is ready to read the headnotes organized under these topics and key numbers. To find a topic and key number with its headnotes, locate the digest volume that contains the topic. The digest volumes are organized alphabetically by topic. Under each topic, the key numbers are organized in numerical order. The headnotes appear under the key number.

3. Reading the Headnotes Organized under the Relevant Topics and Key Numbers

When West reprints a headnote in a digest, it places that headnote under the relevant topic and key number. If a topic and key number entry in a digest has more than one headnote organized under it, these headnotes will be arranged according to the court that decided the case. In state digests, federal cases are listed first, with state cases following. In regional digests, cases are grouped by state. Within each court system, the cases are then listed by hierarchy of court. The highest appellate court is listed first, followed by any intermediate appellate court, and, finally, the trial court. Further, cases from each court are listed in reverse chronological order. To make this organization obvious, West prints a court abbreviation and date at the beginning

Table 7-3. Selected Court Abbreviations in *Arizona Digest* Entries

Court Name	Digest Abbreviation
Supreme Court of Arizona	Ariz.
Court of Appeals of Arizona	Ariz.App.Div. 1 Ariz.App.Div. 2 Ariz.App.
Tax Court of Arizona	Ariz.Tax
United States Supreme Court	U.S.(Ariz.)
United States Circuit Court of Appeals	C.C.A.9(Ariz.)
United States District Court	D.Ariz.

of each headnote. A key to these abbreviations can be found in the front of each digest volume. Table 7-3 shows some of the court abbreviations used in *Arizona Digest*.

Do not rely on digest headnotes as legal authority. Instead, use the citation to the case at the end of the headnote to locate the case and read the case. A headnote may also contain citations to any statutes that appear in the case.

If a jurisdiction has not decided a case on the topic and key number being researched, there will be no entries under that topic and key number in the digest. Because all West digests use the same topics and key numbers, once a legal researcher finds a relevant topic and key number for a legal issue, the researcher can look up that topic and key number in any other West digest to find persuasive authority.

4. Updating the Research

Updating digest research ensures that a legal researcher has located citations to the current cases on a legal point. The first place to look for current case citations is (1) any pocket part in the back of the digest volume for your topic and key number or (2) in any soft-bound, interim pamphlet behind the digest volume for your topic and key number. Then look at the end of the digest series for a single pamphlet containing updates to all volumes; this is called the cumulative supplementary pamphlet. Pocket parts and pamphlets are organized in the same way as the bound digest volume. If there are new cases, they will be listed under the topic and key number. If there are no new cases, there will be no entry for the topic and key number and, most likely, the topic and key number will not even be included in the pocket part or pamphlet. Finally, if West has made changes to its topics and key numbers (e.g., creation of a new key number), these changes will be indicated in the pocket part or pamphlet. This possibility provides another reason to update digest research.

There is a final step for updating beyond the soft-bound pamphlets. The closing tables in the soft-bound pamphlet indicate the ending reporter volume through which it is current. Look at all the relevant reporter volumes and advance sheets published after this ending reporter volume to see if cases on a research topic have been published. A mini-digest of cases in each reporter is printed in the back of the reporter for this purpose. If there is a need to locate more current research (cases published in the last 24 hours), use LexisNexis, Westlaw, or free Internet sources.

C. Using the Digest System with a Case or Party Name

You many begin a research project knowing either the name of a relevant case or the name of a party in the case. Use the Table of Cases in the digest to locate the case citation using these names. This table lists cases alphabetically by both the primary plaintiff's name and by the primary defendant's name. Like other portions of the digest, the Table of Cases is updated using pocket parts.

D. Using the Digest System's "Words and Phrases"

Some research projects require you to find legal definitions of terms. Courts sometimes define terms, especially when a statute has left a term undefined or in an area of common law. Digests provide references to these legal definitions in a "Words and Phrases" index. Simply look up the term in the Words and Phrases volumes. Relevant cases will be listed, along with a short summary of the definition. Words and Phrases volumes are updated with pocket parts.

II. Electronic Media

Both pay research databases and free Internet sources provide ways to search for cases when the legal researcher does not have a relevant citation. As pointed out in Chapter 6, however, free Internet sources are generally searchable only by parties' names, dates, and docket numbers. Free Internet sources do not allow a search of the body of the case, and do not provide any finding aids to use, such as the West topics and key number system. Thus, most legal researchers rely on LexisNexis and Westlaw when searching for cases online.

A. LexisNexis

There are three ways to search for relevant case citations in Lexis-Nexis: word searching, subject-specific searching, and segment searching. Appendix 7-1 at the end of this chapter shows how a case appears online in LexisNexis.

1. Word Searching

To perform a word search, first choose a database to search. LexisNexis databases are available for individual jurisdictions as well as for various compilations of jurisdictions. For instance, Arizona cases can be found in the databases detailed in Table 7-4.

As with choosing a print digest, it is most effective—as to time and cost—to choose the narrowest database that will give relevant results. Thus, to find an Arizona federal district court case on wiretapping, choose the "AZ Federal and State Cases" database. After choosing the relevant database, construct a word search as explained in Chapter 1.

2. Subject Searching

LexisNexis provides the availability to search for cases by subject. Under the "Search" tab, click on "by Topic or Headnote." An alphabetical list of legal subjects will appear. Scroll through these topics

Table 7-4. LexisNexis Databases Containing Arizona Cases

LexisNexis Database	Coverage
Federal and State Cases, Combined	All federal and state cases
AZ Federal and State Cases	Arizona state and federal cases
AZ Cases, Administrative Decisions & Attorney General Decisions, Combined	Arizona state cases, Arizona attorney general decisions, and administrative decisions
AZ State Cases, Combined	Arizona state cases
AZ Supreme Court Cases from 1866	Arizona Supreme Court cases from 1866
AZ Court of Appeals Cases from 1965	Arizona Court of Appeals cases from 1965

and click on any subject to expand the list. If there is a relevant subject, click on the subject to bring up a search screen. At this point, LexisNexis invites input for which database to search and for any restrictions to the research, such as necessary terms or date restrictors. The search will locate cases in the chosen jurisdiction that fall under the subject chosen and that meet any additional restrictions requested.

A search for other cases can also be made by subject directly from a case. After reading a case on a relevant subject and wanting to find other cases on that subject, click on the "More Like This Headnote" link following the headnotes located at the top of each case in Lexis-Nexis. The next screen allows restriction by jurisdiction and dates, then the resulting search lists cases with the same LexisNexis headnote. These headnotes do not correspond to West headnotes but are unique to LexisNexis.

3. Segment Searching

In many instances, a legal researcher may know some information about a case that will help narrow the search. For example, a legal researcher may know the citation, the parties' names, the judge's name, or the date the case was decided. It is possible to search these components of a case by utilizing the segment searching feature on Lex-isNexis. Once a database is chosen, the search screen gives the option to search by segments such as date, court, judge, citation, core terms (terms chosen by LexisNexis to represent the case's subject), and at-torney, among others. These segment options are listed directly below the search box. Click on a relevant segment and type in the known information as a word search in the adjacent blank space. Clicking the tab for "Add" will add the segment search to the original search box. A legal researcher can add as many segment searches as needed. LexisNexis then searches only the selected segments in each case in the database.

B. Westlaw

Westlaw also has three ways to search for relevant case citations: word searching, subject-specific searching, and field searching. These mirror the LexisNexis search techniques explained earlier. See Appendix 7-2 at the end of this chapter for an example of a case as it appears on Westlaw.

1. Word Searching

As with LexisNexis, begin a word search on Westlaw by choosing a database to search. Databases containing Arizona cases are detailed in Table 7-5. Again, try to choose the narrowest database that will produce relevant results. Thus, to find an Arizona Supreme Court case on punitive damages awarded for fraud claims, choose the "AZ-CS" database. After choosing the relevant database, construct a word search as explained in Chapter 1.

Table 7-5. Westlaw Databases Containing Arizona Cases

Westlaw Database	Coverage
ALLCASES	All federal and state cases
CT9-ALL	Ninth Circuit federal and state cases
AZ-CS-ALL	Arizona state and federal cases
AZ-CS	Arizona state cases

2. Subject Searching

Although it is not apparent on the computer screen, Westlaw organizes cases in its databases just as it organizes them in the print digests and reporters. This means that a legal researcher can search Westlaw using topics and key numbers by using the Custom Digest just as the legal researcher would search the print-media digests. The Custom Digest feature is located under the "Key Numbers and Digest" option in the pull-down "More" window at the top of the screen. Digest topics are listed alphabetically. A legal researcher can scroll through these topics and click on any topic to expand the list to include the relevant key numbers. Clicking on a relevant key number brings up a search screen. Choose which database to search and add any other restrictions to the research, such as necessary terms or date restrictors. This search will locate cases in the selected jurisdiction that are indexed under that topic and key number and that meet any additional restrictions requested.

The Custom Digest feature can be accessed directly from a case. Specifically, after reading a case and finding a topic and key number that are relevant to the research question, click on the relevant key number link right in the headnotes to the case to get to the Custom Digest search screen. Alternatively, click on the link for "Most Cited Cases."

Another type of subject searching in Westlaw is the KeySearch feature. The KeySearch feature contains an alphabetical list of research subjects, which may then be further subdivided into more specific subjects. This list is not identical to the Custom Digest list. KeySearch initially contains a smaller, broader list of research subjects than the Custom Digest does, because KeySearch combines related topics and key numbers. Clicking on a KeySearch subject brings up a search screen. At this point, choose which jurisdiction to search and add any other restrictions.

3. Field Searching

Field searching is similar to segment searching on LexisNexis. Choose a database, and the search screen provides the option to search the database by fields. These field options are listed directly below the search box and include citation, the parties' names, the judge's name, and the date the case was decided. Click on a relevant field option to add a word search to be conducted in that field. Westlaw can search multiple fields at one time.

Appendix 7-1. Sample Arizona Case on LexisNexis, part 1

Reproduced by permission of LexisNexis. Further reproduction of any kind is strictly prohibited.

Appendix 7-1. Sample Arizona Case on LexisNexis, part 2

was a statutory prerequisite to consideration for an award. Rather, relative financial disparity between the parties was the benchmark for eligibility. If the trial court found such a disparity, it was then authorized to undertake its discretionary function of determining whether an award was appropriate. In doing so, the trial court could consider the fact that the applicant spouse had the ability to pay. The arbitrator's findings established the wife's entitlement to fees, and there was no direct evidence to support the husband's contention that the arbitrator improperly used the award as a tool to better equalize the division of property.

OUTCOME: The court affirmed the trial court's order requiring the husband to pay additional attorneys' fees to the wife. The court also awarded the wife her reasonable attorneys' fees on appeal.

CORE TERMS: arbitrator's, spouse, disparity, attorneys' fees, abilities to pay, award of fees, financial resources, inability to pay, marriage, unable to pay, able to pay, relevant factor, eligibility, predicate, eligible, dissolution proceeding, award of attorneys' fees, statutory interpretation, abuse of discretion, apportioned, earning, poorer, recommended, decree, fees incurred, fees award, dissolution action, division of property, duty of support, reasonableness

LEXISNEXIS? HEADNOTES   ⊟ **Hide**

Civil Procedure > Appeals > Reviewability > General Overview 🗂
Civil Procedure > Appeals > Standards of Review > De Novo Review 🗂
Civil Procedure > Appeals > Standards of Review > Fact & Law Issues 🗂
HN1 The court of appeals reviews an issue of statutory interpretation independently. More Like This Headnote

Civil Procedure > Remedies > Costs & Attorney Fees > Costs > General Overview 🗂
HN2 See Ariz. Rev. Stat. ? 25-324 (2000). *Shepardize: Restrict By Headnote*

Civil Procedure > Remedies > Costs & Attorney Fees > Attorney Expenses & Fees > General Overview 🗂
HN3 An applicant's inability to pay his or her own attorneys' fees is not a prerequisite to consideration for an award under Ariz. Rev. Stat. ? 25-324 (2000). Rather, relative financial disparity between the parties is the benchmark for eligibility. If the trial court finds such a disparity, it is then authorized to undertake its discretionary function of determining whether an award is appropriate. In doing so, the court can include in its consideration the fact that the applicant spouse has the ability to pay, but cannot grant or deny an award on this basis alone. Rather the court must consider all relevant factors. More Like This Headnote |

Reproduced by permission of LexisNexis. Further reproduction of any kind is strictly prohibited.

Appendix 7-1. Sample Arizona Case on LexisNexis, part 3

alone. Rather the court must consider all relevant factors. More Like This Headnote |
Shepardize: Restrict By Headnote

COUNSEL: John Friedeman, P.C., Phoenix, By John Friedeman, Attorneys for Appellant.

Lynn M. Pearlstein, Ltd., Phoenix, By Lynn M. Pearlstein, Attorneys for Appellee.

JUDGES: James B. Sult, Presiding Judge. CONCURRING: G. Murray Snow, Judge, Maurice Portley, Judge.

OPINION BY: James B. Sult

OPINION

[**1048] [*589] SULT, Judge

P1 Peter Magee, Husband, appeals from an order of the trial court requiring him to pay attorneys' fees incurred by his wife, Martha Magee, in post-decree proceedings in the parties' dissolution action. According to Husband, the award is not authorized under Arizona Revised Statutes ("A.R.S.") ? 25-324 (2000) because Wife did not show that she was unable to pay her own fees, which Husband contends is the statutory predicate for consideration for an award. We disagree that A.R.S. ? 25-324 **[***2]** requires a showing of actual inability to pay as a predicate for consideration, and we conclude that all a spouse need show is that a relative financial disparity in income and/or assets exists between the spouses. Because that disparity exists between these parties, the trial court properly found that Wife was eligible for consideration, and the court consequently **[**1049] [*590]** was authorized to determine whether, in the exercise of its discretion, an award should be made. Because the award actually made by the court was appropriate in the circumstances presented, we affirm.

BACKGROUND

P2 After Wife filed a petition to dissolve her marriage to Husband, the parties agreed to submit all issues to arbitration and the trial court assigned the case to an arbitrator. After considering the evidence, the arbitrator submitted recommended findings of fact and conclusions of law on all issues. The trial court adopted the arbitrator's findings and conclusions and entered a decree that included an award to Wife of $ 10,000 in attorneys' fees.

P3 The parties thereafter filed several motions objecting to the terms of the decree. Following further proceedings, the arbitrator twice **[***3]** submitted amended findings and conclusions to the trial

Reproduced by permission of LexisNexis. Further reproduction of any kind is strictly prohibited.

Appendix 7-2. Sample Arizona Case on Westlaw, part 1

H	**Magee v. Magee**
	206 Ariz. 589, 81 P.3d 1048
	Ariz.App. Div. 1,2004.
	January 08, 2004 (Approx. 1 page)

FOR EDUCATIONAL USE ONLY
West Reporter Image (PDF)

206 Ariz. 589, 81 P.3d 1048, 416 Ariz. Adv. Rep. 7

Court of Appeals of Arizona,
Division 1, Department A.
In re the Marriage of Martha Hale MAGEE, Petitioner-Appellee,
v.
Peter MAGEE, Respondent-Appellant.
No. 1 CA-CV 03-0199.
Jan. 8, 2004.

Background: Husband and wife engaged in post-decree proceedings in dissolution action. The Superior Court, Maricopa County, Cause No. DR 99-001577, A. Craig Blakey, II, J., ordered husband to pay additional attorney fees incurred by wife. Husband appealed.

Holdings: The Court of Appeals, Sult, J., held that:
(1) attorney fees statute requires showing only of financial disparity between husband and wife, rather than one spouse's actual inability to pay fees, and
(2) additional award of fees was proper exercise of discretion in this case.

Affirmed.

West Headnotes

[1] KeyCite Notes

30 Appeal and Error
   30XVI Review
     30XVI(H) Discretion of Lower Court
       30k984 Costs and Allowances
         30k984(5) k. Attorneys' Fees. Most Cited Cases

Court of Appeals reviews an award of attorney fees to determine whether it constituted an abuse of discretion.

[2] KeyCite Notes

134 Divorce
   134V Alimony, Allowances, and Disposition of Property
     134k220 Allowance for Counsel Fees and Expenses
       134k224 k. Grounds. Most Cited Cases

Statute allowing award of attorney fees in dissolution actions requires showing only of financial disparity between husband and wife, rather than one spouse's actual inability to pay fees; requiring payment of spouse's fees is derived and justified from duty to support, which is not conditioned on receiving spouse's being destitute. A.R.S. § 25-324.

Reprinted with permission of West, a Thomson business.

Appendix 7-2. Sample Arizona Case on Westlaw, part 2

[3] KeyCite Notes

⟜134 Divorce
  ⟜134V Alimony, Allowances, and Disposition of Property
    ⟜134k220 Allowance for Counsel Fees and Expenses
      ⟜134k224 k. Grounds. Most Cited Cases

Although one spouse's ability to pay attorney fees in a dissolution action does not disqualify that spouse from being awarded attorney fees, ability to pay is one factor the court may consider when exercising its discretionary function of determining whether an award of fees is appropriate. A.R.S. § 25-324.

[4] KeyCite Notes

⟜134 Divorce
  ⟜134V Alimony, Allowances, and Disposition of Property
    ⟜134k220 Allowance for Counsel Fees and Expenses
      ⟜134k224 k. Grounds. Most Cited Cases

Additional award of $25,000 in attorney fees to wife in post-dissolution-decree proceeding was proper exercise of discretion, where husband's financial resources were substantially greater than wife's, both parties had taken reasonable positions in proceeding, and nothing indicated that fee award was tool to equalize the division of property. A.R.S. § 25-324.

**1048 *589 John Friedeman, P.C. By John Friedeman, Phoenix, Attorneys for Appellant.

Lynn M. Pearlstein, Ltd. By Lynn M. Pearlstein, Phoenix, Attorneys for Appellee.

OPINION

SULT, Judge.
¶ 1 Peter Magee, Husband, appeals from an order of the trial court requiring him to pay attorneys' fees incurred by his wife, Martha Magee, in post-decree proceedings in the parties' dissolution action. According to Husband, the award is not authorized under Arizona Revised Statutes ("A.R.S.") § 25-324 (2000) because Wife did not show that she was unable to pay her own fees, which Husband contends is the statutory predicate for consideration for an award. We disagree that A.R.S. § 25-324 requires a showing of actual inability to pay as a predicate for consideration, and we conclude that all a spouse need show is that a relative financial disparity in income and/or assets exists between the spouses. Because that disparity exists between these parties, the trial court properly found that Wife was eligible for consideration, and the court consequently **1049 *590 was authorized to determine whether, in the exercise of its discretion, an award should be made. Because the award actually made by the court was appropriate in the circumstances presented, we affirm.

BACKGROUND

¶ 2 After Wife filed a petition to dissolve her marriage to Husband, the parties agreed to submit all issues to arbitration and the trial court assigned the case to an arbitrator. After considering the evidence, the arbitrator submitted recommended findings of fact and conclusions of law on all issues. The trial court adopted the arbitrator's findings and conclusions and entered a decree that included an award to Wife of $10,000 in attorneys' fees.

¶ 3 The parties thereafter filed several motions objecting to the terms of the decree. Following further proceedings, the arbitrator twice submitted amended findings and conclusions to the trial court. Among other modifications, the arbitrator proposed amending his original finding regarding a prenuptial agreement that had been entered into by the parties the day before their marriage. The arbitrator had initially determined that this agreement had expired during the third year of the marriage, but amended that determination to find that the agreement continued in force throughout the marriage. This amendment resulted in some assets being re-designated as Husband's separate property, which in

Reprinted with permission of West, a Thomson business.

Chapter 8

Researching Administrative Law

Administrative law is the general term for rules promulgated by state and federal agencies. According to Arizona statute, a rule is "an agency statement of general applicability that implements, interprets or prescribes law or policy, or describes the procedure or practice requirements of an agency." [1] Simply put, a legislature creates an agency to enforce a statutory scheme. Once created, the agency becomes part of the executive, or enforcement, branch of the government, although an agency may be given functions other than just promulgating rules.

Specifically, a legislature creates an agency by passing legislation known as an enabling act. An *enabling act* sets forth the explicit powers of the agency. These powers may include the right to create rules, the right to hear controversies, and the right to grant licenses, among other powers. Agencies cannot act outside of their enabling act authority. Thus, to research the powers of an agency, start by researching the agency's enabling act.

Agencies must also comply with any relevant state administrative procedures act. For example, Arizona state agencies must comply with the Arizona Administrative Procedures Act (AAPA).[2] The AAPA provides guidelines for promulgating rules, including the manner for getting public input in the rule-making, as well as the timeframe and manner for rule-making. One unique feature of the AAPA is its creation of the Governor's Regulatory Review Council (GRRC). Any agency that is not exempt must submit any notice of rule-making and the eventual final rule (along with a required statement of the rule's

---

1. Ariz. Rev. Stat. Ann. § 41-1001(17) (2004).
2. Ariz. Rev. Stat. Ann. § 41-1001-1092.11 (2004).

economic, small business, and consumer impact) to GRRC for approval. When an agency submits a final rule to GRRC, GRRC has 90 days to approve the rule and statement or to return the rule and statement to the agency for changes. In addition, every five years, an agency must review its current rules to determine if any of these rules need to be changed or repealed, and the agency must then file with GRRC a report summarizing its findings.

If an agency is given the power to promulgate rules (also known as regulations in some jurisdictions, most notably the federal system), these rules are primary authority. In fact, rules often look just like statutes in their layout. Although rules operate like statutes for the purpose of legal analysis, statutes have authority over rules when considering weight of authority. Like statutes and proposed statutes, rules and proposed rules are available in both print and electronic media.

I. Researching Arizona Administrative Law

The steps for researching Arizona administrative law are outlined in Table 8-1. A sample Arizona rule appears in Appendix 8-1 at the end of this chapter.

The first step is an optional step and is needed only if the research issue involves determining the scope of an agency's powers. To find

Table 8-1.
Outline of the Research Process for Arizona Administrative Law

Step 1: Research the enabling act, if the research problem involves the scope of the agency's authority.

Step 2: Locate the rule in *Arizona Administrative Code* using the title index or an online search.

Step 3: Update the rule in *Arizona Administrative Register*, unless using LexisNexis or Westlaw (which regularly update rules).

Step 4: Search for cases and administrative decisions applying the relevant rule.

Step 5: Review the agency's website for additional information.

an agency's enabling act, use the agency's name as a keyword to research *Arizona Revised Statutes Annotated.* Chapter 4 explains the process for researching *Arizona Revised Statutes Annotated.* Once the enabling act is located in the *Arizona Revised Statutes Annotated,* look for any cases that have interpreted or addressed the enabling act. These cases will generally be listed in the annotations following the enabling act, although it may be necessary to research cases as explained in Chapters 6 and 7.

A. *Arizona Administrative Code*

The Arizona Secretary of State publishes *Arizona Administrative Code,* commonly known as *A.A.C.,* which contains all the official rules of Arizona's agencies in a ten-volume set. This print-media set is the official compilation of rules, although the Arizona Secretary of State also publishes *A.A.C.* on its website at www.azsos.gov/public _services/rules.htm.

The Arizona Secretary of State publishes supplements to *A.A.C.* every three months. The print-media version must contain the proper supplements in order for it to be current. The Arizona Secretary of State's website contains a schedule of supplement publication dates for this purpose.

The version of *A.A.C.* available on the Arizona Secretary of State's website is not updated every three months; it is generally updated only once per year. Thus, a legal researcher must look at the print supplements to make sure a rule has not been changed. The Arizona Secretary of State publishes the date through which *A.A.C.* is current on the *A.A.C.* webpage.

In most instances, a statute's annotation will contain a citation to any relevant agency rules, as explained in Chapter 4.[3] A legal researcher who has a citation simply has to locate the rule by looking

---

3. Chapter 1 explains that an effective way to approach research is to look for applicable annotated statutes before administrative law and case law.

first for the volume containing the rule's title and chapter number and then looking for the relevant section. For example, the citation to Ariz. Admin. Code § 9-6-708 means the rule is in Volume 9 under Title 6 and Chapter 708.

Without a citation to a relevant rule, browse the title index located in the first volume of the print-media *A.A.C.* This index is sub-divided into titles and chapters. The chapters correspond to individual agencies, and the agency's rules are listed numerically under each chapter. There is no comprehensive subject index. Similarly, if researching *A.A.C.* on the Arizona Secretary of State's website, browse the title index and the rules themselves; the rules are not searchable by keyword.

The advantage of researching *A.A.C.* on the pay research databases, such as LexisNexis and Westlaw, is that the rules are searchable by a word search. In addition, both LexisNexis and Westlaw incorporate any supplements to *A.A.C.* as soon as the supplements are published. These are pay research databases, however, so use of these services should be guided by the strategies explained in Chapter 1. The LexisNexis database is "AZ - Arizona Administrative Code," and the Westlaw database is "AZ-ADC."

B. *Arizona Administrative Register*

The Arizona Secretary of State also publishes *Arizona Administrative Register*. Known as *A.A.R.*, it contains all information relevant to rule-making activities including docket openings, proposed rules, final rules, exempt rules, emergency rules, summary rules, notices of public information, and oral proceedings (public meetings) on proposed rulemakings. *A.A.R.* is available in print media and in electronic media, similar to *A.A.C.*

The Arizona Secretary of State publishes *A.A.R.* weekly both in print and on its website at www.azsos.gov/public_services/rules.htm.[4] Each *A.A.R.* volume contains an index to the rules appearing in that

---

4. The Arizona Secretary of State also publishes a semi-annual index every six months. This index contains the rules affected within the six-month period, as well as summaries of Attorney General opinions and the Gover-

volume; this index is organized by titles and chapters, and the rules are listed in numerical order under each chapter. This index is not cumulative. Thus, to see if a rule has any proposed changes, check the index of each *A.A.R.* volume published after the publication date of the current *A.A.C.*

LexisNexis and Westlaw also contain *A.A.R.*, and each database is searchable by word search. Updates to the rules are automatically added to the *A.A.R.* databases, which is one benefit of using Lexis-Nexis and Westlaw. The LexisNexis database is "AZ State Regulation Tracking," and the Westlaw database is "AZ-REG-NET."

C. Other Sources for Arizona Administrative Law

Many Arizona agencies place their rules on their agency websites. In addition, an agency may provide other types of guidance, such as its internal policies and governing documents. A list of Arizona agencies with links to their websites is available on the Arizona State Legislature website at http://az.gov/webapp/portal/alpha.jsp?name=agency. Never consider administrative law research complete unless the agency's website has been checked.

Some agencies hear contested cases, and an administrative law judge may write a decision in the case. Table 8-2 lists Arizona agencies (or an agency's department or board) that hear contested cases.

Administrative law judge decisions are available from the Arizona Office of Administrative Hearings on its website at www.azoah.com. The website has specific instructions for researching decisions and for researching other information, such as the hearing calendar and judge biographies.

A final source of administrative law is any case that has interpreted an Arizona agency rule. Research cases by conducting a word search using the actual rule as part of the research terms. Word searches and case law research are explained in Chapters 1, 6, and 7.

---

nor's Executive Orders. This index is available both in print media and on the Arizona Secretary of State's website.

Table 8-2. Arizona Agencies that Hear Contested Cases

- Department of Corrections
- Board of Executive Clemency
- Industrial Commission
- Arizona Corporation Commission
- Board of Regents
- Personnel Board
- Department of Juvenile Corrections
- Department of Transportation
- Department of Economic Security
- Department of Revenue
- Board of Tax Appeals
- Board of Equalization
- Department of Education
- Board of Fingerprinting

II. Researching Federal Administrative Law

Federal administrative law is made in a manner similar to Arizona administrative law, although the rules made by federal agencies are called regulations. Similar to researching Arizona law, the first step in researching federal administrative law may be to find the agency's enabling act, if the research project questions an agency's authority to act. This process is similar to the process described for researching Arizona administrative law, explained earlier. Also analogous to Arizona agencies, federal agencies must comply with the federal Administrative Procedures Act.[5]

Federal regulations and proposed regulations are available in both print and electronic media.

A. *Code of Federal Regulations*

The Government Printing Office (GPO) publishes *Code of Federal Regulations* (*C.F.R.*) in both print media and on its website at

---

5. 5 U.S.C. § 551 *et seq.* (2000).

www.gpoaccess.gov/cfr/index.html. *C.F.R.* contains all regulations published by federal agencies and is organized into 50 titles based on those agencies.[6] The GPO updates *C.F.R.* in both print media and on its website only once per year on a rolling schedule: Titles 1-16[7] are updated by January 1, Titles 17-27 are updated by April 1, Titles 28-41 are updated by July 1, and Titles 41-50 are updated by October 1. Although these updates are not always immediately available, it is easy to see the year of updating for a *C.F.R.* title in print media based on the color of its cover. The GPO prints each year's *C.F.R.* in a different color.

An easy way to begin researching federal regulations is to look for regulatory citations after the body of a relevant statute in an annotated federal code, such as *U.S.C.S.* or *U.S.C.A.*, as explained in Chapter 4.[8] Locate the regulation by looking first for its *C.F.R.* title and then for the relevant section number within that title.

To begin research with no citation to a relevant regulation, use *C.F.R.*'s general index, which is located at the end of the print-media set. This index contains subject keywords and agency names, so research terms will help with this step. The version of *C.F.R.* located on GPO's website is also searchable by keyword, title, and citation. To update any *C.F.R.* section located in print media or on the GPO's website, use the booklet or link called *List of C.F.R. Sections Affected* (*L.S.A.*). The *L.S.A.* provides information on all *C.F.R.* sections affected since the last publication of *C.F.R.* Then check *Federal Register* for any days beyond the publication date of the *L.S.A.* This process is explained in section II.B below.

Like *A.A.C.*, moreover, *C.F.R.* is available on LexisNexis at "CFR - Code of Federal Regulations" and on Westlaw at "CFR." One reason to use these pay research databases is that the regulations are automatically updated without any extra research steps.

---

6. These 50 titles do not necessarily match the 50 titles of the *U.S.C.*, although many *C.F.R.* titles and *U.S.C.* titles do match in number and subject.

7. Title 3, "The President," is the only exception to this updating schedule, as it is not updated annually.

8. Because an annotated statute provides such helpful references, it is important to look for statutes first, as explained in Chapter 1.

B. *Federal Register*

Federal Register is the federal government's daily report of agency activities. *Federal Register* contains notices of proposed regulations, notices of public comments and hearings on proposed regulations, and final regulations, among other helpful content. The GPO publishes *Federal Register* daily in soft-bound booklets as well as daily on its website at www.gpoaccess.gov/fr/index.html. To find if a regulation is reported in *Federal Register*, use the table in the back of each *Federal Register* called "CFR Parts Affected in this [Month]." It is also helpful to browse each issue of *Federal Register* on the GPO's website for this same information or perform a keyword search.

Federal Register is available on LexisNexis at "FR - Federal Register" and on Westlaw at "FR."

C. Other Sources for Federal Administrative Law

Like the Arizona agencies, many federal agencies also have their own websites and publish their own rules and governing documents. Administrative law research is not complete until a legal researcher has looked at the agency's website. A list of federal agencies is available at www.whitehouse.gov/government/independent-agencies.html.

The final step is to locate cases interpreting a federal regulation. This process is explained earlier in section I.C of this chapter.

III. Arizona Attorney General Opinions

The Arizona Attorney General provides legal advice to the State of Arizona, its agencies, and state officials acting in their official capacities. In other words, the Arizona Attorney General is the state's lawyer. The Arizona Attorney General also investigates and prosecutes consumer fraud, white-collar crime, organized crime, public corruption, drug-related crimes, environmental violations, and civil rights violations.

The legislature or any Arizona public officer, including a county attorney, can ask the Arizona Attorney General for an opinion on a legal matter. Opinions of the Arizona Attorney General are advisory and do not have the same precedential effect as a case. A private citizen cannot ask the Arizona Attorney General for advice.

Arizona Attorney General opinions are available on the Arizona Attorney General's website at www.azag.gov/opinions. Opinions are available from 1999 through the present. They are not searchable, but they are organized by year. To find opinions older than 1999, contact a law library for access to the Arizona Attorney General pamphlets containing these opinions. The first part of the citation to an opinion indicates the year the opinion was issued (in the last two digits), and the next three numbers merely show the order in which the opinions were issued. For example, the citation No. 107-006, indicates that this opinion was the sixth opinion given by the Attorney General in 2007.

Appendix 8-1.
Sample Arizona Rule from *Arizona Administrative Code*

R9-6-708. Release of Immunization Information

In addition to the persons who have access to immunization information according to A.R.S. § 36-135(D) and consistent with the limitations in A.R.S. § 36-135(E) and (H), the Department may release immunization information to:

1. An authorized representative of a state or local health agency for the control, investigation, analysis, or follow-up of disease;

2. A child care administrator, to determine the immunization status of a child in the child care;

3. An authorized representative of WIC, to determine the immunization status of children enrolled in WIC;

4. An individual or organization authorized by the Department, to conduct medical research to evaluate medical services and health related services, health quality, immunizations data quality, and efficacy; or

5. An authorized representative of an out-of-state agency, including a state health department, local health agency, school, child care,

health care provider, or a state agency that has legal custody of a child.

Historical Note

Adopted effective January 28, 1987 (Supp. 87-1). Renumbered to Section R9-6-309 effective October 19, 1993 (Supp. 93-4). New Section R9-6-708 renumbered from R9-6-707 and amended by final rulemaking at 8 A.A.R. 4274, effective September 16, 2002 (Supp. 02-3).

Chapter 9

Researching Arizona Tribal Law

I. Introduction to Tribal Law and Federal Indian Law

Tribal law is the law that Indian tribes use to govern themselves as sovereign bodies. This law may include a tribal constitution, a tribal code, and tribal case law. *Federal Indian law* is the law dealing primarily with the status of the Indian tribes and their special relationship to the federal government.[1] This law may include treaties, statutes, administrative law, executive orders, and case law. Because researching federal Indian law involves the same steps for researching other federal law, as explained in Chapters 3 through 8, this chapter will deal with the special considerations involved when researching tribal law.

In Arizona, there are twenty-two Indian tribes with a combined population of over 250,000, which is approximately five percent of Arizona's total population.[2] Reservations and tribal lands cover over one-fourth of the land in Arizona. These tribes are listed in Appendix 9-1. Most lawyers in Arizona should expect that their practices will include issues of tribal law and federal Indian law, whether they practice real estate law, water law, or general litigation.

---

1. Title 25 of *United States Code* is the relevant title for federal Indian law.
2. Arizona Commission on Indian Affairs, *Tribal Demographics*, www .indianaffairs.state.az.us/tribes/demo.html (last updated Mar. 28, 2005).

II. Tribal Treaties, Constitutions, and Codes

Tribal law is difficult to research because many tribes do not distribute their codes or case law in the same manner as states do. Some tribes developed their law primarily in the oral tradition, while others have written law. Thus, the best place to begin tribal law research is always with the tribe itself. Some tribes have websites to facilitate research. Appendix 9-1 at the end of this chapter gives website addresses and contact information for Arizona tribal courts, as well as research notes.

If there is no official tribal website, or the closest law library does not carry tribal law materials, there are other sources for researching tribal law. The most comprehensive source is the National Indian Law Library, which is a public law library devoted to tribal law, as well as federal Indian law. The National Indian Law Library provides tribal law information on its website at http://narf.org/nill. Clicking on the "Tribal Law Gateway" link brings up search links for tribal treaties, constitutions, codes, and case law.[3] Most of the categories are searchable by tribe or by subject. There is also an alphabetical listing of all Indian tribes, with websites for their constitutions and codes.

III. Tribal Case Law

To search specifically for tribal case law, check both the National Indian Law Library and the local law library's catalog for tribal law reporters. The two most notable tribal law reporters are *Indian Law Reporter* and *Navajo Reporter*. *Indian Law Reporter* is a loose-leaf binder that is updated every month with new pamphlets. The pamphlets are divided into the following categories:

---

3. Both LexisNexis and Westlaw provide searchable access to treaties.

- United States Supreme Court opinions and proceedings
- United States Court of Appeals opinions
- United States District Court opinions
- United States Court of Federal Claims opinions
- State Court opinions
- Tribal Court opinions
- Miscellaneous proceedings
- Table of Cases and Topical Index

Similarly, the *Navajo Reporter* is a loose-leaf binder that is periodically updated with new pages. It contains an alphabetical listing of cases as an index, but it has no topical index or digest system.

Two free Internet sources also provide searchable tribal case law, as well as other sources of tribal law:

- National Tribal Justice Resource Center
  www.ntjrc.org/legal/opfolder/default.asp
- Tribal Court Clearinghouse
  www.tribal-institute.org.

Both the National Tribal Justice Resource Center and Tribal Court Clearinghouse provide searchable access to tribal case law for the Fort McDowell Yavapai Nation Tribal Court, the Hopi Tribal Court, and the Navajo Nation courts. The National Tribal Justice Court Clearinghouse will soon add access to the Gila River Community Court case law.

Some pay research databases also provide access to tribal case law. VersusLaw.com has a good collection of tribal case law and is searchable; it provides access to decisions from the Fort McDowell Yavapai Nation Tribal Court (1999–present), the Hopi Tribal Court (1981–present), and the Navajo Nation courts (1970–present). Neither Westlaw nor LexisNexis currently provides access to tribal case law for tribes located in Arizona. Westlaw does provide searchable access to some tribal case law, such as the Oklahoma Tribal Court Reports. LexisNexis provides searchable access to tribal case law from tribes located in Montana. When researching tribal case law, it is a good idea to check all three services—VersusLaw, Westlaw, and LexisNexis—to see what is currently included in each.

IV. Secondary Sources

Some secondary sources may prove helpful in researching tribal law. *Tribal Law Journal* is an Internet-only journal available at http://tlj.unm.edu. In addition, *Encyclopedia of Native American Legal Tradition*[4] and *Introduction to Tribal Legal Studies*[5] are two helpful treatises devoted to tribal law. Both LexisNexis and Westlaw provide searchable access to *American Indian Law Review*.

Appendix 9-1. Arizona Tribal Court Information

Ak-Chin Indian Community Court
Phone: (520) 568-1385
Official tribal website: www.ak-chin.nsn.us/main.html

Cocopah Tribal Court
Phone: (928) 627-2550
Official tribal website: www.cocopah.com

Colorado River Indian Tribal Court
Phone: (928) 669-1355
Official tribal website: http://critonline.com

Fort McDowell Yavapai Nation Tribal Court
Phone: (480) 816-7604
Official tribal website: www.ftmcdowell.org
• Tribal code is available on official tribal website
• Tribal case law published at *National Tribal Law Justice Resource Center*, at *Tribal Law Clearinghouse*, and on VersusLaw.com

Fort Mohave Tribal Court
Phone: (928) 346-5293
Official tribal website: www.fortmojave.com

Fort Yuma-Quechan Tribal Court
Phone: (760) 572-5552
Informational website: www.itcaonline.com/tribes_quechan.html

---

4. Bruce Elliot Johansen, *Encyclopedia of Native American Legal Tradition* (Greenwood Press 1998).

5. Justin B. Richland & Sarah Deer, *Introduction to Tribal Legal Studies* (AltaMira Press 2004).

Gila River Indian Community Court
Phone: (520) 562-1983/9270
Official tribal website: www.gric.nsn.us/newdirection
• Tribal case law published at *National Tribal Law Justice Resource Center*, at *Tribal Law Clearinghouse*, and on VersusLaw.com

Havasupai Tribal Court
Phone: (928) 448-2701
Official tribal website: www.havasupaitribe.com/index.htm

Hopi Tribal Court
Phone: (928) 738-5561
Informational website: www.itcaonline.com/tribes_hopi.html
• Tribal case law published at *National Tribal Law Justice Resource Center*, at *Tribal Law Clearinghouse*, and on VersusLaw.com

Hualapai Tribal Court
Phone: (928) 769-2538/2338
Informational website: www.itcaonline.com/tribes_hualapai.html

Kaibab-Paiute Tribal Court
Phone: (928) 643-7214
Official tribal website: www.kaibabpaiutetribal.com

Navajo Nation Courts
Phone: (928) 871-6763 (Navajo Nation Supreme Court)
Official tribal website: www.navajo.org
• Tribal code and other information available at www.navajocourts.org
• Tribal case law published in *Navajo Reporter* and at *National Tribal Law Justice Resource Center*, at *Tribal Law Clearinghouse*, and on VersusLaw.com

Pascua Yaqui Tribal Court
Phone: (520) 883-5000
Official tribal website: www.pascuayaquitribe.org
• Tribal code is available on official tribal website

Salt River Pima-Maricopa Indian Community Court
Phone: (480) 850-8115
Official tribal website: www.saltriver.pima-maricopa.nsn.us

San Carlos Apache Tribal Court
Phone: (928) 475-2648
Official tribal website: www.sancarlosapache.com/home.htm

San Juan Southern Paiute Tribal Court
Phone: (928) 283-5539
Informational website: www.itcaonline.com/tribes_sanjuan.html

Tohono O'Odham Nation Justice Center
Phone: (520) 383-6300
Informational website: www.itcaonline.com/tribes_tohono.html

Tonto Apache Tribal Court
Phone: (928) 474-8625
Informational website: www.itcaonline.com/tribes_tonto.html

White Mountain Apache Tribal Court
Phone: (928) 338-4346
Official tribal website: www.wmat.us
• Tribal code is available on official tribal website

Yavapai-Apache Tribal Court
Phone: (928) 567-1033
Official tribal website: www.yavapai-apache.org

Yavapai-Prescott Tribal Court
Phone: (928) 771-3300
Official tribal website: www.ypit.com

Zuni Tribal Court
Phone: (505) 782-7045
Official tribal website: www.ashiwi.org
• Legislation and constitution are available on official tribal website

Chapter 10

Updating Research

Updating is a process of (1) learning which subsequent authorities refer to a case, statute, or rule on which your legal analysis relies and (2) determining whether those subsequent authorities have any impact on the validity of that legal analysis. Updating legal research is an important step in every research project. Not only does updating research ensure reliance only on valid law, but it may also lead to other primary or secondary authorities that you may have missed during the research process. For this reason, many legal researchers choose to update their research continually throughout a research project and not just at the end of it.

When using print media, the first way to update the research is to check the back of the print volumes for pocket parts. Check also at the end of the volumes for any soft-bound pamphlet that may provide updates. Next, use a print citator, such as *Shepard's Citations*. A *citator*'s purpose is to report what comments primary and secondary sources have made about other primary and secondary sources. These reports indicate whether a case has been reversed, overruled, or changed in some way. A citator may also indicate whether a constitution, statute, or rule has been repealed or amended, or is in the process of being amended.

Although citators are available in print media, most libraries and law firms are not carrying them anymore for two reasons: (1) they are expensive and (2) they are not as current as electronic media because of the natural lag time built into the printing process. A Shepard's report on LexisNexis is current within about 24 hours and can be modified to suit specific research needs. Westlaw's KeyCite is updated as soon as a source is added to Westlaw. Both have the added advantage of flexibility: they can be modified to suit specific research needs.

This chapter will explain how to use the electronic media citators on LexisNexis (Shepard's) and Westlaw (KeyCite). The updating process is similar for all sources, although the contents of each source's updating report differ.

I. Shepard's

There are two ways to retrieve the Shepard's report for a legal authority. The first way is to click on the tab for "Shepard's" on the LexisNexis research page and enter the citation of the source being checked. The second way is to click on the Shepard's signal on the top of the page displaying the constitutional provision, statute, case, or administrative rule. Table 10-1 shows the meaning of Shepard's signals for cases on LexisNexis.

For clarity, the rest of this discussion assumes that the authority being updated is a case. Additional information for other authorities that can be Shepardized is included in footnotes.

Table 10-1. Shepard's Signals for Cases on LexisNexis

Shepard's Signal	Meaning
Green diamond with a plus sign	The case has received positive treatment (e.g., affirmed).
Blue circle	The case has been cited and has received treatment that is nether positive nor negative (the letter "A" is used with this symbol) or no treatment or history code is assigned to the case (the letter "I" is used with this symbol).
Yellow triangle	The case has received treatment that may be construed as negative (e.g., distinguished).
Orange square with letter "Q"	The case has been questioned, but it has not been overruled or reversed.
Red stop sign	The case has been overruled, reversed, or treated extremely negatively.

A Shepard's report is a page of citations. These citations are the sources that have cited the case being updated. To choose a report that includes all of the case's history as well as any citing sources, choose the "Shepard's for Research" option under the search box on the Shepard's page or choose the "Full" option from any Shepard's report page. In a full Shepard's report, the first part of the report will show a summary of the Shepard's report, including the Shepard's signal, a list of the types of comments made by the citing sources (e.g., distinguished, explained, followed), and how many sources made this type of comment, as well as a catalog of the LexisNexis headnotes that are commented upon by the citing sources. After this summary, the citation of the case being updated will appear. Following this citation will be any direct history for the case. *Direct history* for cases shows how other cases in this same lawsuit have been decided. Generally, direct history will indicate whether a case being updated has been amended, affirmed, reversed, or vacated.[1]

The last part of the full report will list the primary and secondary sources that cite the case being updated. Federal sources by jurisdiction are listed first, followed by state sources by jurisdiction, and, then, secondary sources. Both the direct history list and the citing sources list contain citations to the citing sources, as well as links to the pinpoint page with the relevant commentary. Appendix 10-1 at the end of this chapter shows a sample full Shepard's report for an Arizona case.

If a legal researcher is interested only in finding out if a case is still good law, the legal researcher can click on the option for "Shepard's for Validation" under the search box on the Shepard's page or on "KWIC" on a Shepard's report page. The KWIC report will show only the subsequent history and citing references with analysis for the case. Appendix 10-2 at the end of this chapter shows a KWIC Shepard's report for an Arizona case.

By using the tabs at the top of the Shepard's report page, a legal researcher can restrict a report to list only sources that positively com-

---

1. Direct history for constitutions, statutes, and administrative rules shows how the actions of the legislature or agency have affected the source being updated. This history shows whether the constitutional provision, statute, or administrative rule being updated has been amended or repealed.

ment on the source being updated or only sources that negatively comment on the source being updated. Other restrictions are available by using the "FOCUS" function and choosing the restriction that best fits the research needs. For example, LexisNexis allows a legal researcher to restrict a search by date, jurisdiction, or LexisNexis headnote. Restricting a report is particularly helpful when the Shepard's report is long.

Whether using a full Shepard's report or a restricted report, remember not to rely solely on a Shepard's symbol when updating a source. For instance, a red stop sign may be used to indicate that a point of law in a case has been overruled, but that case may have six points of law and the other five points are still good law. The only way to know this is (1) to read the report and take notes of the cases that negatively affect the original case and (2) to link to and read those citing cases to see how much of the original case they affect.

II. KeyCite

KeyCite is a separate function on the Westlaw homepage. In order to update a source, click on the tab for "KeyCite" on the homepage and enter the citation of the source being updated. Some computers contain a list of "Shortcuts" in the left Westlaw frame, which has a search box for KeyCite; again, simply enter the citation. KeyCite can also be used directly from a case, constitutional provision, statute, or administrative rule. Click on the KeyCite status flag on the top of the page displaying the case, constitutional provision, statute, or administrative rule in order to enter the KeyCite function. Table 10-2 shows the meaning of KeyCite's status flags for cases.

Similar to Shepard's for Validation, a KeyCite "Full History" report is a list of citations of the direct history of the case. Direct history shows how other cases in this same lawsuit have been decided.[2] Direct history indicates whether a source is still valid.

---

2. Direct history also shows how actions of the legislature or agency have affected constitutions, statutes, and administrative rules.

Table 10-2. KeyCite Status Flags on Westlaw

KeyCite Status Flags	Meaning
Green letter "C"	The case has citing references but does not have any direct or indirect history.
Blue letter "H"	The case has some history, but that history is not negative.
Yellow flag	The case has negative history, but the case has not been overruled or reversed.
Red flag	The case has history that indicates it is no longer good law for at least one point in the case.

The last part of a KeyCite full history report will list the negative indirect history for the source being checked, if there is any. Appendix 10-3 at the end of the chapter shows an example of a KeyCite full history report for an Arizona case.

To find all primary and secondary sources that cite the case being updated (not just the history of the case), modify the KeyCite report by clicking on the tab titled "Citing References." All of the same information from the original KeyCite full history report will be listed first, followed by federal sources by jurisdiction, then state sources by jurisdictions, and, lastly, secondary sources and court documents. As the name of the report suggests, a citing references report contains citations to the citing sources, as well as links to the pinpoint page with the relevant commentary. Appendix 10-4 at the end of the chapter shows an example of a citing references KeyCite report for an Arizona case.

As shown in Appendix 10-4 at the end of the chapter, these citing references citations may be preceded by a series of one to four stars. The number of stars in the series indicates how in-depth the citing source discussed the original source. Table 10-3 shows the definitions of the various numbers of stars.

Two additional features in KeyCite play an important role in research. First, KeyCite reports contain references to relevant West headnotes in each citing source. Second, KeyCite reports provide links to portions of citing sources that quote the original source

Table 10-3. KeyCite Stars on Westlaw

Number of KeyCite Stars	Meaning
☆☆☆☆	The source has a particularly long discussion of the case (more than one page).
☆☆☆	The source has a considerable discussion of the case (between one paragraph and one page).
☆☆	The source has some discussion of the case (around one paragraph).
☆	The source only briefly references the case, perhaps in a string citation.

through the use of an oversize quotation mark symbol that may appear after an entry on a KeyCite report (see Appendix 10-4 to this chapter). Clicking on these quotation marks links directly to the portion of the citing source where the original source is quoted.

In addition, KeyCite provides graphical views of the direct history of each case.[3] Use the links at the side of the KeyCite report to open the graphical view. The graphical view of a case shows a table that is divided horizontally into the three levels of court (trial, intermediate appellate, and highest appellate). Each court level is highlighted in a different color. The case citation is placed on the appropriate level (with the trial court on the bottom and the highest court on the top), along with the direct history case citations. Read the table from left to right to indicate the passage of time and from bottom to top to indicate the case's travels through the court system. Using a graphical view of a case's direct history is particularly helpful when a case has had complex appellate history.

A KeyCite report can be limited by using the "Limit KeyCite Display" button in the bottom left of the right-hand frame. Options include limiting the report by date, jurisdiction, headnote, and type of document. Use the "Locate" option to restrict a KeyCite report by a particular word or phrase.

---

3. KeyCite reports for statutes also include a graphical view. This graphical view shows any earlier versions of the statute, as well as future amendments to the statute, all on one easy-to-read page.

As with Shepard's signals, do not to rely solely on any KeyCite symbol when updating a source. The only way to know what a citing source says about the source being updated is to read it. This is especially true of any case that indicates negative treatment of the source being updated.

Appendix 10-1, part 1
Sample Excerpt from Full Shepard's Report for an Arizona Case

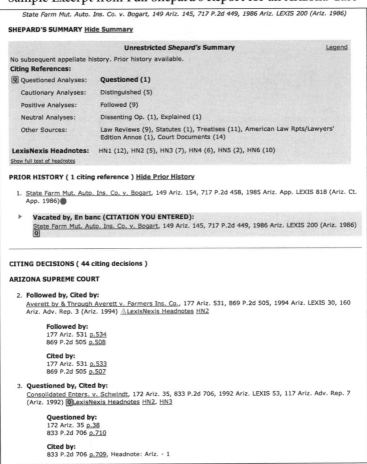

Reproduced by permission of LexisNexis. Further reproduction of any kind is strictly prohibited.

Appendix 10-1, part 2
Sample Excerpt from Full Shepard's Report for an Arizona Case

4. **Followed by:**

Fremont Indem. Co. v. New Eng. Reinsurance Co., 168 Ariz. 476, 815 P.2d 403, 1991 Ariz. LEXIS 58, 92 Ariz. Adv. Rep. 6 (Ariz. 1991)△

168 Ariz. 476 p.478
168 Ariz. 476 p.481
815 P.2d 403 p.405
815 P.2d 403 p.408, Headnote: Ariz. - 5

5. **Cited by:**

Schultz v. Farmers Ins. Group of Cos., 167 Ariz. 148, 805 P.2d 381, 1991 Ariz. LEXIS 12, 79 Ariz. Adv. Rep. 3 (Ariz. 1991) △LexisNexis Headnotes HN1

167 Ariz. 148 p.152
805 P.2d 381 p.385

6. **Cited by:**

Rashid v. State Farm Mut. Auto. Ins. Co., 163 Ariz. 270, 787 P.2d 1066, 1990 Ariz. LEXIS 17, 54 Ariz. Adv. Rep. 3 (Ariz. 1990) △LexisNexis Headnotes HN6

163 Ariz. 270 p.273
163 Ariz. 270 p.275
787 P.2d 1066 p.1069
787 P.2d 1066 p.1071

7. **Cited by:**

Brown v. State Farm Mut. Auto. Ins. Co., 163 Ariz. 323, 788 P.2d 56, 1989 Ariz. LEXIS 231, 49 Ariz. Adv. Rep. 18 (Ariz. 1989) △LexisNexis Headnotes HN1, HN3, HN6

163 Ariz. 323 p.325
788 P.2d 56 p.58

8. **Cited by:**

State Farm Mut. Auto. Ins. Co. v. Wilson, 162 Ariz. 251, 782 P.2d 727, 1989 Ariz. LEXIS 179, 48 Ariz. Adv. Rep. 3 (Ariz. 1989)△

162 Ariz. 251 p.256
782 P.2d 727 p.732

Reproduced by permission of LexisNexis. Further reproduction of any kind is strictly prohibited.

Appendix 10-2, part 1
Sample KWIC Shepard's Report for an Arizona Case

State Farm Mut. Auto. Ins. Co. v. Bogart, 149 Ariz. 145, 717 P.2d 449, 1986 Ariz. LEXIS 200 (Ariz. 1986)

SHEPARD'S SUMMARY Hide Summary

Unrestricted *Shepard's* Summary: KWIC Legend

No subsequent appellate history. Prior history available.

Citing References:

[Q] Questioned Analyses:	**Questioned (1)**
Cautionary Analyses:	Distinguished (5)
Positive Analyses:	Followed (9)
Neutral Analyses:	Dissenting Op. (1), Explained (1)
LexisNexis Headnotes:	HN1 (4), HN2 (5), HN3 (3), HN4 (2), HN6 (3)

Show full text of headnotes

CITING DECISIONS (15 citing decisions)

ARIZONA SUPREME COURT

1. **Followed by, Cited by:**
   Averett by & Through Averett v. Farmers Ins. Co., 177 Ariz. 531, 869 P.2d 505, 1994 Ariz. LEXIS 30, 160 Ariz. Adv. Rep. 3 (Ariz. 1994) ⚠ LexisNexis Headnotes HN2

   Followed by:
   177 Ariz. 531 p.534

2. **Questioned by, Cited by:**
   Consolidated Enters. v. Schwindt, 172 Ariz. 35, 833 P.2d 706, 1992 Ariz. LEXIS 53, 117 Ariz. Adv. Rep. 7 (Ariz. 1992) [Q] LexisNexis Headnotes HN2, HN3

   Questioned by:
   172 Ariz. 35 p.38

3. **Followed by:**
   Fremont Indem. Co. v. New Eng. Reinsurance Co., 168 Ariz. 476, 815 P.2d 403, 1991 Ariz. LEXIS 58, 92 Ariz. Adv. Rep. 6 (Ariz. 1991) ⚠

   168 Ariz. 476 p.478
   168 Ariz. 476 p.481

ARIZONA COURT OF APPEALS

4. **Distinguished by, Cited by:**
   Allstate Ins. Co. v. Great Am. Ins. Cos., 197 Ariz. 448, 4 P.3d 991, 2000 Ariz. App. LEXIS 37, 316 Ariz. Adv. Rep. 57, 120 No. 12 Ariz. Bus. Gaz. 7 (Ariz. Ct. App. 2000) ⚠ LexisNexis Headnotes HN1, HN3

   Distinguished by:
   197 Ariz. 448 p.450

5. **Distinguished by:**
   State Farm Mut. Auto. Ins. Co. v. Arrington, 192 Ariz. 255, 963 P.2d 334, 1998 Ariz. App. LEXIS 86, 270 Ariz. Adv. Rep. 28, 118 No. 31 Ariz. Bus. Gaz. 7 (Ariz. Ct. App. 1998) ◆ LexisNexis Headnotes HN2

   192 Ariz. 255 p.260

Reproduced by permission of LexisNexis. Further reproduction of any kind is strictly prohibited.

Appendix 10-2, part 2
Sample KWIC Shepard's Report for an Arizona Case

6. **Followed by:**
   John Deere Ins. Co. v. West Am. Ins. Group, 175 Ariz. 215, 854 P.2d 1201, 1993 Ariz. App. LEXIS 103, 140 Ariz. Adv. Rep. 11 (Ariz. Ct. App. 1993) ⓘLexisNexis Headnotes HN6

   175 Ariz. 215 p.217

7. **Distinguished by:**
   Consolidated Enters. v. Schwindt, 171 Ariz. 452, 831 P.2d 828, 1991 Ariz. App. LEXIS 42, 81 Ariz. Adv. Rep. 37 (Ariz. Ct. App. 1991) ●LexisNexis Headnotes HN3

   171 Ariz. 452 p.454

8. **Cited in Dissenting Opinion at, Cited by:**
   Fremont Indem. Co. v. New Eng. Reinsurance Co., 165 Ariz. 521, 799 P.2d 862, 1990 Ariz. App. LEXIS 131, 58 Ariz. Adv. Rep. 74 (Ariz. Ct. App. 1990) ●LexisNexis Headnotes HN1, HN4

   Cited in Dissenting Opinion at:
   165 Ariz. 521 p.524

9. **Followed by, Explained by:**
   State Farm Mut. Auto. Ins. Co. v. Dimmer, 160 Ariz. 453, 773 P.2d 1012, 1988 Ariz. App. LEXIS 355, 22 Ariz. Adv. Rep. 16 (Ariz. Ct. App. 1988) ◆LexisNexis Headnotes HN2, HN6

   Followed by:
   160 Ariz. 453 p.459

   Explained by:
   160 Ariz. 453 p.458

10. **Followed by:**
    Green v. Mid-America Preferred Ins. Co., 156 Ariz. 265, 751 P.2d 581, 1987 Ariz. App. LEXIS 611 (Ariz. Ct. App. 1987)⚠

    156 Ariz. 265 p.268

7TH CIRCUIT - U.S. DISTRICT COURTS

11. **Followed by:**
    GuideOne Mut. Ins. Co. v. Papa John's USA, Inc., 2005 U.S. Dist. LEXIS 8914 (S.D. Ind. Apr. 10, 2005) LexisNexis Headnotes HN4

    2005 U.S. Dist. LEXIS 8914

Appendix 10-3.
Sample Full History KeyCite Report for an Arizona Case

Graphical History

State Farm Mut. Auto. Ins. Co. v. Bogart
149 Ariz. 145, 717 P.2d 449
Ariz.,1986.
March 27, 1986

History
(Showing 6 documents)

Direct History

SELECT TO PRINT, EMAIL, ETC.

1 State Farm Mut. Auto. Ins. Co. v. Bogart, 149 Ariz. 154, 717 P.2d 458 (Ariz.App. Div. 1 Jan 17, 1985) (NO. 1 CA-CIV 6554)

   Opinion Vacated by

2 KeyCited Citation:
   State Farm Mut. Auto. Ins. Co. v. Bogart, 149 Ariz. 145, 717 P.2d 449 (Ariz. Mar 27, 1986) (NO. 18116-PR)

Negative Citing References (U.S.A.)

Superseded by Statute as Stated in

3 Consolidated Enterprises, Inc. v. Schwindt, 171 Ariz. 452, 831 P.2d 828 (Ariz.App. Div. 2 Feb 28, 1991) (NO. 2 CA-CV 90-0244), review granted (Jun 11, 1991) ★ ★ ★ **HN: 1 (P.2d)**

4 Consolidated Enterprises, Inc. v. Schwindt, 172 Ariz. 35, 833 P.2d 706 (Ariz. Jul 16, 1992) (NO. CV-91-0171-PR) ★ ★ ★ **HN: 1 (P.2d)**

C 5 RSUI Indem. Co. v. Associated Electric & Gas Ins. Services Ltd., 2007 WL 1526433 (D.Ariz. May 23, 2007) (NO. CV 05-2962-PHX-JAT) ★ ★

Abrogation Recognized by

6 Korzun v. Chang-Keun Yi, 207 W.Va. 377, 532 S.E.2d 646 (W.Va. May 05, 2000) (NO. 26634) ★ ★ ★ **HN: 1,2 (P.2d)**

Reprinted with permission of West, a Thomson business

Appendix 10-4, part 1
Sample Excerpt from Citing References
KeyCite Report for an Arizona Case

🖼️ **Graphical History**   🏳   **State Farm Mut. Auto. Ins. Co. v. Bogart**
149 Ariz. 145, 717 P.2d 449
Ariz.,1986.
March 27, 1986

FOR EDUCATIONAL USE ONLY

Citing References
(Showing 108 documents)

Negative Cases (U.S.A.)

📢 SELECT TO PRINT, EMAIL, ETC.

Superseded by Statute as Stated in

☐ **C** 1 RSUI Indem. Co. v. Associated Electric & Gas Ins. Services Ltd., 2007 WL 1526433, *2+ (D.Ariz. May 23, 2007) (NO. C 05-2962-PHX-JAT) 🎧 ★ ★

☐ ▷ 2 Consolidated Enterprises, Inc. v. Schwindt, 833 P.2d 706, 709+, 172 Ariz. 35, 38+ (Ariz. Jul 16, 1992) (NO. CV-91-0171-PR) 🎧 ★ ★ ★ **HN: 1 (P.2d)**

☐ ► 3 Consolidated Enterprises, Inc. v. Schwindt, 831 P.2d 828, 830+, 171 Ariz. 452, 454+ (Ariz.App. Div. 2 Feb 28, 1991) (NO. 2 CA-CV 90-0244) ★ ★ ★ **HN: 1 (P.2d)**

Abrogation Recognized by

☐ ▷ 4 Korzun v. Chang-Keun Yi, 532 S.E.2d 646, 649+, 207 W.Va. 377, 380+ (W.Va. May 05, 2000) (NO. 26634) 🎧 ★ ★ ↑ **HN: 1,2 (P.2d)**

Positive Cases (U.S.A.)
★ ★ ★ ★ **Examined**

☐ ▷ 5 Fremont Indem. Co. v. New England Reinsurance Co., 815 P.2d 403, 405+, 168 Ariz. 476, 478+ (Ariz. Jul 23, 1991) (NO. CV-90-0186-PR) 🎧 **HN: 3,4,5 (P.2d)**

☐ ▷ 6 Green v. Mid-America Preferred Ins. Co., 751 P.2d 581, 584+, 156 Ariz. 265, 268+ (Ariz.App. Div. 1 Dec 03, 1987) (NO 1 CA-CIV 9287) 🎧 **HN: 3,4 (P.2d)**

☐ ▷ 7 AMHS Ins. Co. v. Mut. Ins. Co. of Arizona, 258 F.3d 1090, 1095+, 00 Cal. Daily Op. Serv. 6390, 6390+, 2001 Daily Journal D.A.R. 7853, 7853+ (9th Cir.(Ariz.) Jul 30, 2001) (NO. 99-15703, 99-15704) 🎧 **HN: 3,4,5 (P.2d)**

Reprinted with permission of West, a Thomson business

Appendix 10-4, part 2
Sample Excerpt from Citing References
KeyCite Report for an Arizona Case

★ ★ ★ **Discussed**

☐ ▷ **8** Averett v. Farmers Ins. Co. of Arizona, 869 P.2d 505, 507+, 177 Ariz. 531, 533+ (Ariz. Mar 03, 1994) (NO. CV-92-0015-PR) **HN: 3 (P.2d)**

☐ **H 9** Brown v. State Farm Mut. Auto. Ins. Co., 788 P.2d 56, 58+, 163 Ariz. 323, 325+ (Ariz. Dec 14, 1989) (NO. CV-89-0162-PR) **HN: 3,4,5 (P.2d)**

☐ ▷ **10** Arizona Property & Cas. Ins. Guar. Fund v. Herder, 751 P.2d 519, 521+, 156 Ariz. 203, 205+ (Ariz. Feb 25, 1988) (NC CV-87-0081-PR) **HN: 3,4,5 (P.2d)**

☐ **H 11** Allstate Ins. Co. v. Great American Ins. Companies, 4 P.3d 991, 992+, 197 Ariz. 448, 449+, 316 Ariz. Adv. Rep. 57, 57+ (Ariz.App. Div. 1 Mar 07, 2000) (NO. 1 CA-CV 99-0374) **HN: 3,4,5 (P.2d)**

☐ **H 12** Do by Minker v. Farmers Ins. Co. of Arizona, 828 P.2d 1254, 1257+, 171 Ariz. 113, 116+ (Ariz.App. Div. 2 Dec 19, 1991) (NO. 2 CA-CV 91-0083) **99 HN: 4 (P.2d)**

☐ ▷ **13** State Farm Mut. Auto. Ins. Co. v. Dimmer, 773 P.2d 1012, 1017+, 160 Ariz. 453, 458+ (Ariz.App. Div. 1 Nov 29, 1988) (NO. 1 CA-CIV 9794) **HN: 4 (P.2d)**

☐ **H 14** Twin City Fire Ins. Co. v. Fireman's Fund Ins. Co., 386 F.Supp.2d 1272, 1278+, 18 Fla. L. Weekly Fed. D 964, 964+ (S.D.Fla. Sep 12, 2005) (NO. 03-62136-CIV-SEITZ, 03-62143-CIV-SEITZ) **99**

★ ★ **Cited**

☐ ▷ **15** Schultz v. Farmers Ins. Group of Companies, 805 P.2d 381, 385, 167 Ariz. 148, 152 (Ariz. Jan 24, 1991) (NO. CV-90-0221-SA/AP) **HN: 3,5 (P.2d)**

☐ ▷ **16** Rashid v. State Farm Mut. Auto. Ins. Co., 787 P.2d 1066, 1069+, 163 Ariz. 270, 273+ (Ariz. Feb 08, 1990) (NO. CV-89-0219-PR) **HN: 3,4,5 (P.2d)**

☐ **H 17** State Farm Mut. Auto. Ins. Co. v. Wilson, 782 P.2d 727, 732, 162 Ariz. 251, 256, 58 USLW 2251, 2251 (Ariz. Oct 12, 1989) (NO. CV-89-0071-PR)

☐ ▷ **18** Gordinier v. Aetna Cas. & Sur. Co., 742 P.2d 277, 283+, 154 Ariz. 266, 272+ (Ariz. Jul 28, 1987) (NO. CV-86-0609-P

☐ **H 19** State Farm Mut. Auto. Ins. Co. v. Fireman's Fund Ins. Co., 717 P.2d 858, 860+, 149 Ariz. 179, 181+ (Ariz. Mar 27, 1986) (NO. 18201-PR)

☐ **C 20** American Family Mut. Ins. Co. v. Continental Casualty Co., 23 P.3d 664, 666, 200 Ariz. 119, 121, 342 Ariz. Adv. Rep. 13, 13 (Ariz.App. Div. 1 Feb 27, 2001) (NO. 1 CA-CV 00-0020)

☐ **H 21** State Farm Mut. Auto. Ins. Co. v. Arrington, 963 P.2d 334, 339, 192 Ariz. 255, 260, 270 Ariz. Adv. Rep. 28, 28 (Ariz.App. Div. 1 May 26, 1998) (NO. 1 CA-CV 97-0448)

☐ ▷ **22** A.H. By and Through White v. Arizona Property and Cas. Ins. Guar. Fund, 943 P.2d 738, 744, 189 Ariz. 378, 384 (Ariz.App. Div. 1 Oct 29, 1996) (NO. 1 CA-CV 96-0049)

☐ ▷ **23** Nahom v. Blue Cross and Blue Shield of Arizona, Inc., 885 P.2d 1113, 1119+, 180 Ariz. 548, 554+ (Ariz.App. Div. 1 N 22, 1994) (NO. 1 CA-CV 92-0495, 1 CA-CV 93-0018) **HN: 4,5 (P.2d)**

☐ **C 24** John Deere Ins. Co. v. West American Ins. Group, 854 P.2d 1201, 1203+, 175 Ariz. 215, 217+ (Ariz.App. Div. 1 Jun 03, 1993) (NO. 1 CA-CV 91-0437)

☐ ▷ **25** Fremont Indem. Co. v. New England Reinsurance Co., 799 P.2d 862, 864+, 165 Ariz. 521, 523+ (Ariz.App. Div. 2 Apr 10, 1990) (NO. 2 CA-CV 89-0237)

☐ **C 26** Nationwide Mut. Ins. v. CNA Ins. Co., 767 P.2d 716, 718, 159 Ariz. 368, 370 (Ariz.App. Div. 2 Oct 18, 1988) (NO. 2 CA-CV 88-0193) **99**

☐ **C 27** Robson v. Hartford Ins. Group, 751 P.2d 563, 565, 156 Ariz. 247, 249 (Ariz.App. Div. 2 Nov 10, 1987) (NO. 2 CA-CV 87-0141)

☐ **C 28** United Fence Co., Inc. v. Great-West Life Assur. Co., 723 P.2d 722, 726, 150 Ariz. 373, 377 (Ariz.App. Div. 1 Jul 15, 1986) (NO. 1 CA-CIV 8651)

☐ ▷ **29** Coconino County v. Fund Administrators Ass'n, Inc., 719 P.2d 693, 698, 149 Ariz. 427, 432 (Ariz.App. Div. 1 May 08, 1986) (NO. 1 CA-CIV 7684)

☐ **H 30** U.S. Fidelity & Guaranty Co. v. Riggs, 121 F.3d 719, 719 (9th Cir.(Ariz.) Jul 28, 1997) (Table, text in WESTLAW, NO. 96-15405) **HN: 4 (P.2d)**

Reprinted with permission of West, a Thomson business

Appendix A

Legal Citation

To convince another lawyer or a judge that an argument has been thoroughly researched and that the ideas are well supported, a legal researcher must provide references to the authorities used to develop the legal analysis and reach the conclusion. These references are called *legal citations*. They tell the reader where to find the authorities relied on and indicate the level of analytical support the authorities provide.[1] In a legal document, every legal rule and every explanation of the law must be cited. Table A-1 summarizes the purposes of legal citations.

Legal citations are included in the text of legal documents rather than being saved for a bibliography. While it may initially seem that these citations clutter a document, legal citations provide valuable information; an experienced legal reader appreciates legal citations in a document.

The format used for legal citations, however, requires meticulous attention to such riveting details as whether a space is needed between two abbreviations. In this respect, citation format rules can be like fundamental writing rules, which are based on convention, not reason. Why capitalize the personal pronoun "I" but not "we" or "you" or "they"? Why does a comma signify a pause, while a period indicates a stop? Rather than trying to understand why citations are formatted the way they are, the most practical approach is simply to learn citation rules and apply them. Frequent repetition will make them second nature.

---

1. ALWD & Darby Dickerson, *ALWD Citation Manual* 3 (3d ed., Aspen 2006) ("*ALWD Manual*").

Table A-1. Purposes of Legal Citations

- Show the reader where to find the cited materials in the original case, statute, rule, article, or other authority.

- Indicate the weight and persuasiveness of each authority, for example, by specifying the court that decided the case, the author of a document, and the publication date of the authority.

- Convey the type and degree of support the authority offers, for example, by indicating whether the authority supports the point directly or only implicitly.

- Demonstrate that the analysis in the document is the result of careful research.

Source: *ALWD Manual*

Of the many different citation systems that exist, this chapter addresses the two national citation manuals, the *ALWD Citation Manual: A Professional System of Citation*[2] and *The Bluebook: A Uniform System of Citation*.[3] In law practice, state statutes, court rules, and style manuals may dictate the form of citation used before the courts of different states. Arizona does not have a style manual and has not formally adopted either of the national citation manuals as its preferred one.

In addition, each law office or legal agency may have its own preferences for citation or make minor variations to generally accepted format. Some law offices have their own style manuals, drawn from state rules and national manuals. In practice, adjust your citation format to the preferred style. In school, learn the style of the teacher for class or the style of the law journal for scholarly writing. After becoming aware of the basic function and format of citation, adapting to a slightly different set of rules will not be difficult.

---

2. *Id.*

3. *The Bluebook: A Uniform System of Citation* (The Columbia Law Review et al. eds., 18th ed., The Harvard Law Review Assn. 2005).

I. The *ALWD Manual*

The *ALWD Manual* is the best manual for novices because it uses a single system of citation for legal memoranda, court documents, law review articles, and all other legal documents. The explanations are clear, and the examples are useful to both law students and practicing attorneys.[4]

A. Incorporating Citations into a Document

Each idea that comes from a case, statute, article, or other source must be followed by a citation. Thus, paragraphs that state legal rules and explain the law should contain many citations. ALWD 320-21, Rule 43.2.[5]

A citation may offer support for an entire sentence or for an idea expressed in part of a sentence. If the citation supports the entire sentence, place it in a separate *citation sentence* that begins with a capital letter and ends with a period. ALWD 317, Rule 43.1(a). If the citation supports only a portion of the sentence, include it immediately after the relevant part of that sentence and set it off from the sentence by commas in what is called a *citation clause*. ALWD 317, Rule 43.1(b). Table A-2 shows an example of each.

Do not cite the client's facts or your conclusions about a case, statute, or other authority. The following sentence should not be cited: "Because our client divorced her husband in 2004, she is no longer a surviving spouse." These facts and conclusions are unique to the client's situation and would not be found anywhere in the reference source.

---

4. This manual has been adopted by law professors at many schools. *See* www.alwd.org/cm (last visited November 12, 2007). For a helpful review, see M.H. Sam Jacobson, *The ALWD Citation Manual: A Clear Improvement Over the Bluebook*, 3 J. App. Prac. & Process 139 (2001).
5. Throughout this chapter, references will be provided to *ALWD* and *Bluebook* pages and rule numbers in this fashion.

Table A-2. Examples of a Citation Sentence and a Citation Clause

---

Citation Sentence: If a person is divorced from her spouse, she is no longer a surviving spouse under Arizona law. Ariz. Rev. Stat. Ann. § 14-2802(A) (2000). A surviving spouse is defined to exclude "[a] person who, after an invalid decree or judgment of divorce or annulment obtained by the decedent, participates in a marriage ceremony with a third person." Ariz. Rev. Stat. Ann. § 14-2802(B) (2000).

Citation Clause: Arizona law not only explains the effect of divorce on a spouse's will, Ariz. Rev. Stat. Ann. § 14-2802(A) (2000), but also explains the effect of murdering one's spouse, Ariz. Rev. Stat. Ann. § 14-2803 (2000).

B. Case Citations

A full citation to a case includes (1) the name of the case, (2) the volume and reporter in which the case is published, (3) the first page of the case, (4) the exact page in the case that contains the idea being cited (e.g., the *pinpoint* or *jump cite*), (5) the court that decided the case, and (6) the date the case was decided. ALWD 64-105, Rule 12. The key points in Rule 12 for citation to cases are given below, along with examples.

1. Essential Components of Case Citations

Include the name of just the first party on each side, even if several are listed in the case caption. If the party is an individual, include only the party's last name. If the party is a business or organization, shorten the party's name by using the abbreviations in *ALWD*'s Appendix 3. ALWD 453-61.

Between the parties' names, place a lower case "v" followed by a period. Do not use a capital "V" or the abbreviation "vs." Place a comma after the second party's name.

The parties' names may be italicized or underlined. Use the style preferred in your office or class, and use that style consistently throughout each document. ALWD 64-76, Rule 12.2 (case names);

ALWD 13, Rule 1.1 (typeface choice). Do not combine italics and underlining in one cite or within a single document.

> EXAMPLE: *Matthews v. Chevron Corp.*, 362 F.3d 1172, 1180 (9th Cir. 2004).

Next, give the volume and the reporter in which the case is found. Pay special attention to whether the reporter is in its first, second, or third series. Abbreviations for common reporters are found on page 77 of *ALWD Manual*. Arizona reporters are included on pages 361-62. In the example above, 362 is the volume number and F.3d is the reporter abbreviation for *Federal Reporter, Third Series*.

After the reporter name, include both the first page of the case and the pinpoint page containing the idea that is being referenced, separated by a comma and a space. ALWD 33-36, Rule 5; ALWD 82-83, Rule 12.5. The first page of the *Matthews* case in the example is 1172, and the page where the cited idea came from is page 1180. If the pinpoint page being cited is also the first page of the case, then the same page number will appear twice.[6]

In a parenthetical following this information, indicate the court that decided the case, using abbreviations in *ALWD*'s Appendix 1 (state courts) and Appendix 4 (federal courts). ALWD 83-86, Rule 12.6. In Appendix 1, the abbreviations for the courts of each state are included in parentheses just after the name of the court. In the *Matthews* example, the Ninth Circuit Court of Appeals, a federal court, decided the case.

If the reporter abbreviation clearly indicates which court decided a case, do not repeat this information in the parenthetical. To give an example, only cases of the United States Supreme Court are reported in *United States Reports*, abbreviated U.S. Repeating a court abbrevi-

---

6. When using an online version of a case, remember that a reference to a specific reporter page may change in the middle of a computer screen or a printed page. This means that the page number indicated at the top of the screen or printed page may not be the page where the relevant information is located. For example, if the notation *1181 appeared in the text before the relevant information, the pinpoint cite would be to page 1181, not to page 1180 (the number on the top of the screen or printed page).

ation in citations to that reporter would be duplicative. It is also unnecessary duplication to repeat a portion of a court abbreviation if the reporter abbreviation contains that information, as indicated by the last two examples below. By contrast, *Pacific Reporter, Third Series*, abbreviated P.3d, publishes decisions from different courts within several states, so the court that decided a particular case needs to be included parenthetically. Thus, in the second example below, "Cal." indicates that the decision came from the California Supreme Court rather than from another court whose decisions are also published in this reporter.

> EXAMPLES: *Brown v. Bd. of Educ.*, 349 U.S. 294, 300 (1955).
> *Ketchum v. Moses*, 17 P.3d 735, 736 (Cal. 2001).
> *Harrington v. Pulte Home Corp.*, 211 Ariz. 241, 245 (App. 1 Div. 2005).
> *Nielson v. Patterson*, 204 Ariz. 530, 533 (2003).

In the *Nielson* case example above, no court abbreviation is needed in the date parenthetical. Because Ariz. is the abbreviation for both the reporter (*Arizona Reports*) and the Arizona Supreme Court, there is no need to repeat the abbreviation.

Note that the court abbreviations are not the same as postal codes. Abbreviating the California Supreme Court as either CA or Calif. or abbreviating the Arizona Supreme Court as AZ would be incorrect.

The final piece of required information in most cites is the date the case was decided. For cases published in reporters, give only the year of decision, not the month or date. Do not confuse the date of decision with the date on which the case was argued or submitted, the date on which a motion for rehearing was denied, or the publication date of the reporter. ALWD 86-87, Rule 12.7.

2. Full and Short Citations to Cases

The first time a case is mentioned by name, immediately give its full citation, including all of the information outlined above. ALWD

Table A-3. Examples of Full Citations

Assume that this is the first time the case has been mentioned in this document.

Correct: The intent of the legislature enacting a statute needs to be determined. *Day v. City of Fontana*, 19 P.3d 1196, 1198 (Cal. 2001).

Correct, but should be avoided: In *Day v. City of Fontana*, 19 P.3d 1196, 1198 (Cal. 2001), the court noted that the intent of the legislature in enacting a statute needs to be determined.

52, Rule 11.1; ALWD 519-21, Appendix 6 (sample memorandum). Even though it is technically correct to include the full citation at the beginning of a sentence, a full citation takes up considerable space. By the time a legal reader gets through the citation and to the idea at the end of the sentence, the reader may have lost interest. (See Table A-3.)

After a full citation has been used once to introduce an authority, short citations are subsequently used to cite to this same authority. A short citation provides just enough information to allow the reader to locate the longer citation and find the pinpoint page. ALWD 52-56, Rules 11.2 and 11.3.

When the immediately preceding citation is to the same source and the same page, use *id.* as the short citation. When the second citation is to a different page within the same source, follow the *id.* with "at" and the new pinpoint page number. Capitalize *id.* when it begins a citation sentence, just as the beginning of any sentence is capitalized. ALWD 55, Rule 11.3(d).

If the citation is from a source that is not the immediately preceding citation, give the name of one of the parties (generally, the first party named in the full citation), the volume of the reporter, the reporter abbreviation, and the pinpoint page following "at." ALWD 52-53, Rule 11.2; ALWD 102-03, Rule 12.21(b).

EXAMPLE: Fraud that justifies an annulment must involve the essentials of marriage. *E.g. Wolfe v. Wolfe*, 389 N.E.2d 1143, 1145 (Ill. 1979); *Louis v.*

Louis, 260 N.E.2d 469, 471 (Ill. App. 1st Dist.
1970). A misrepresentation is essential to marriage if it "makes impossible the performance of
the duties and obligations of that marriage."
Wolfe, 398 N.E.2d at 1145. A court takes into
account the facts of each case in deciding what
is essential to marriage. *Id.*

If there is a reference to a case by name in the sentence, the short
citation does not need to repeat the case name, ALWD 103, Rule
12.21(c), though lawyers often do repeat it. The second sentence of
the example would also be correct as follows: According to *Wolfe,* a
misrepresentation is essential to marriage if it "makes impossible the
performance of the duties and obligations of that marriage." 398
N.E.2d at 1145.

The format "*Wolfe* 1145," consisting of just a case name and page
number, is incorrect. The volume, reporter abbreviation, and "at" are
also needed.

3. Prior and Subsequent History

Sometimes a citation needs to show what happened to a case at an
earlier or later stage of litigation. The case being cited may have reversed an earlier case, as in the example below. Or, if for historical
purposes it makes sense to include a discussion of a case that was later
overruled, a legal reader needs to know that as soon as the case is introduced. Prior and subsequent history can be appended to the full
citations discussed above. ALWD 87-92, Rules 12.8-12.10.

EXAMPLE: The only time that the Supreme Court addressed the requirement of motive for an EM-
TALA claim, the court rejected that requirement. *Roberts v. Galen of Va.,* 525 U.S. 249, 253
(1999), *rev'g* 111 F.3d 405 (6th Cir. 1997).

4. Cases Available Electronically Only

In some instances, a case may be available electronically only.
When a case is available only on LexisNexis or Westlaw, the follow-

ing information is needed in the citation: case name as required under ALWD Rule 12.2, database identifier with year and unique document number. ALWD 94–95, Rule 12.12(a).

EXAMPLES: *Haines v. Goldfield Prop. Owners Assn.*, 2006
WL 1160648 (May 1, 2006).
Haines v. Goldfield Prop. Owners Assn., 2006
Ariz. App. LEXIS 91 (May 1, 2006).

Do not follow this rule if the case is available in a reporter, regardless what media is used to access the case.

C. Statutes

1. State Statutes

The general formats for citing specific state statutes are located in *ALWD*'s Appendix 1. For *Arizona Revised Statutes Annotated*, the official code for Arizona, give the code name, a section symbol, the title number, section number, and date.

EXAMPLE: Ariz. Rev. Stat. Ann. § 17-363 (2004).

Many Arizona practitioners do not follow this format, however. They use the abbreviation "A.R.S." for *Arizona Revised Statutes Annotated*, which is Thomson West's abbreviation. Make sure to conform to whatever usage is expected.

There is one unofficial statutory compilation of Arizona's laws, *Arizona Annotated Revised Statutes*, published by LexisNexis. When citing to this compilation, include the publisher information in the date parenthetical.

EXAMPLE: Ariz. Rev. Stat. § 17-363 (Lexis 2004).

2. Federal Statutes

The general rule for citing federal laws is to cite *United States Code* (U.S.C.), which is the official code for federal statutes. In reality, that publication is published so slowly that the current language will most likely be found in an unofficial code, either *United States Code Annotated* (published by Thomson West) or *United States Code*

Service (published by LexisNexis). A citation to a federal statute includes the title, code name, section, publisher (except for *U.S.C.*), and date. The date given in statutory citations is the date of the volume in which the statute is published, not the date the statute was enacted. If the language of a portion of the statute is reprinted in the pocket part, include the dates of both the bound volumes and the pocket part. ALWD 111-15, Rule 14.2. If the language appears only in the pocket part, include only the date of the pocket part, with the abbreviation "Supp." in the date parenthetical. ALWD 45, Rule 8.1.

D. Signals

A citation must show the legal reader that the writer understands the level of support each authority provides. An introductory signal provides this information. ALWD 323-28, Rule 44. The more common signals are explained in Table A-4. Using an explanatory parenthetical is recommended when using a signal.

Table A-4. Common Signals

Signal	Meaning
No signal	The source provides direct support for the idea in the sentence.
	The citation identifies the source of a quotation.
See	The source offers implicit support for the idea in a sentence.
	The source cited offers support in dicta.
See also	The source provides additional support for the idea in the sentence.
	The support offered by *see also* is not as strong or direct as authorities preceded by no signal or by the signal *see*.
E.g.	Many authorities state the idea in the sentence, and you are citing only one as an example; this signal allows you to cite just one source while letting the reader know that many other sources say the same thing.

E. Explanatory Parentheticals

At the end of a citation, a legal writer can append additional information about the authority in parentheses. Sometimes this parenthetical information conveys to the reader the weight of the authority. For example, a case may have been decided *en banc* or *per curiam*. Or the case may have been decided by a narrow split among the judges who heard the case. ALWD 94, Rule 12.11(b). Parenthetical information also allows a writer to name the judges who joined in a dissenting, concurring, or plurality opinion. ALWD 93, Rule 12.11(a). An explanatory parenthetical following a signal can convey helpful, additional information in a compressed space. ALWD 335-37, Rule 46. When using this type of parenthetical, be sure not to inadvertently hide a critical part of the court's analysis at the end of a long citation, where a reader is likely to skip over it.

> EXAMPLE: Excluding relevant evidence during a sentencing hearing may deny the criminal defendant due process. *Green v. Georgia*, 442 U.S. 95, 97 (1979) (per curiam) (regarding testimony of a co-defendant's confession in a rape and murder case).

F. Quotations

Quotations should be used only when the reader needs to see the text exactly as it appears in the original authority. Of all legal audiences, trial courts will probably be most receptive to longer quotations. For example, quoting controlling statutory language can be extremely helpful. As another example, if a well known case explains an analytical point in a particularly insightful way, a quotation may be warranted.

Excessive quotation has two drawbacks. First, quotations interrupt the flow of the writing when the style of the quoted language differs from the writer's style. Second, excessive use of quotations may suggest to the reader that the writer does not fully comprehend the material; it is much easier to cut and paste together a document from pieces of various cases than to synthesize and explain a rule of law. Quotations should not be used simply because it is difficult to think of another way to express an idea.

When a quotation is needed, the words, punctuation, and capitalization within the quotation marks must appear exactly as they are in the original. Treat a quotation as a photocopy of the original text. Any alterations or omissions must be indicated. Include commas and periods inside quotation marks; place other punctuation outside the quotation marks unless it is included in the original text. ALWD 343-44, Rule 47.4(d). Also, try to provide smooth transitions between the original text and the quoted text.

G. Citation Details

- Use proper ordinal abbreviations. The most confusing are 2d for "Second" and 3d for "Third" because they differ from the standard format. ALWD 32, Rule 4.3.
- Do not insert a space between abbreviations of single capital letters. For example, there is no space in U.S. Ordinal numbers like 1st, 2d, and 3d are considered single capital letters for purposes of this rule. Thus, there is no space in P.2d or P.3d because 2d and 3d are considered single capital letters. Leave one space between elements of an abbreviation that are not single capital letters. For example, F. Supp. 2d has a space on each side of "Supp." It would be incorrect to write F.Supp.2d. ALWD 16-17, Rule 2.2.
- In citation sentences, abbreviate case names, court names, months, and reporter names. Do not abbreviate these words when they are part of textual sentences; instead, spell them out as in the example below. ALWD 16-18, Rules 2.1, 2.3; ALWD 453-61, Appendix 3 (months, case names); ALWD 463-70, Appendix 4 (court names); ALWD 404-05, Appendix 1 (federal reporters).

  EXAMPLE: The Ninth Circuit held that Oregon's Measure 11 did not violate constitutional rights provided under the Eighth and Fourteenth Amendments. *Alvarado v. Hill*, 252 F.3d 1066, 1069-70 (9th Cir. 2001).

- It is most common in legal documents to spell out numbers zero through ninety-nine and to use numerals for larger numbers. However, always spell out a number that is the first word of a sentence. ALWD 29-32, Rule 4.2.

II. The *Bluebook*

Student editors of four Ivy League law reviews have developed citation rules that are published as *The Bluebook: A Uniform System of Citation,* now in its eighteenth edition. An author submitting an article for publication in one of those law reviews, or in other law reviews that adhere to *Bluebook* rules, should follow *Bluebook* citation format.

Until the *ALWD Manual* was first published in 2000, the *Bluebook* was the only national citation system that was widely recognized. Many law firms, agencies, and organizations still consider the *Bluebook* citations the norm, although few practicing lawyers know its current rules; most assume that the *Bluebook* rules have not changed since they were in law school. Section II.A below explains how to use the *Bluebook* in writing memoranda and briefs. This section points out some areas of change from earlier editions of the *Bluebook* and some differences between the *ALWD Manual* and the *Bluebook* that a writer may encounter in practice. Section II.B explains how to use the *Bluebook* in writing scholarly articles for publication.

A. *Bluebook* Citations for Practice Documents

For practicing attorneys, the primary difficulty with the *Bluebook* is that it includes two citation systems: one for law review articles and another for legal memoranda and court documents. Most of the *Bluebook*'s 415 pages are devoted to citations used for articles published in law journals. The rules most important to attorneys, those concerning legal memoranda and court documents, are given about forty pages of attention in the *Bluebook*.

Table A-5. Comparison of *ALWD Manual* and *Bluebook* Formats

ALWD Manual All Documents	*Bluebook* Legal Memoranda	*Bluebook* Law Review Articles
Cal. Civ. Pro. Code Ann. § 340.5 (West 2006).	Cal. Civ. Pro. Code § 340.5 (West 2006).	Cal. Civ. Pro. Code § 340.5 (West 2006).

As the example in Table A-5 shows, there is often little or no difference between the final appearance of citations in legal memoranda and court documents using the *Bluebook* and the *ALWD Manual*. However, notice that the *Bluebook* uses a different type—large and small capital letters—for law review citations to the same statute. The following short guide to the *Bluebook* is included to help in locating pertinent material in the *Bluebook*.

1. Quick Reference Guide and the Bluepages

Perhaps the most helpful information in the *Bluebook* is the quick reference guide on the inside back cover of the book, which gives examples of citation used in court documents and legal memoranda.[7] Another helpful portion of the *Bluebook* appears on pages 3 through 43; these are the Bluepages. They provide information for, and additional examples of, citations used in documents other than law review articles. Most basic citation questions and examples are addressed in these forty pages, and these are the pages to consult for writing legal memoranda and court documents.

2. Index

The index at the back of the *Bluebook* is quite extensive, and in most instances it is more helpful than the table of contents. Most often, begin working with the *Bluebook* by referring to the index, if the Bluepages offer no guidance. Page numbers given in regular black type refer to instructions, while those page numbers in blue refer to examples.

---

7. Examples of law review citations are found on the inside front cover.

3. Case Citations

The basic rules for citing cases appear on pages 3 through 13 of the Bluepages. The essential material included in case citations is the same under the *Bluebook* and the *ALWD Manual,* although there are differences in court abbreviations. For example, the *Bluebook* uses "Ariz. Ct. App." to designate the Arizona Court of Appeals, while the *ALWD Manual* uses "Ariz. App. ___ Div." BB 199, T.1; ALWD 361, Appendix 1.

In addition to court abbreviations, the most obvious differences between the two manuals concern abbreviations in Table T.6 on pages 335 through 337 of the *Bluebook.* This list is much shorter than its *ALWD Manual* counterpart. ALWD 453-61. Notably, under the *Bluebook* rule, "United States" is never abbreviated when it is a party's name. BB 7, Rule B.5.1.1(v). Another minor difference between the *Bluebook* and the *ALWD Manual* is the use of apostrophes in abbreviations. The *Bluebook*'s abbreviations use both, while the *ALWD Manual* uses only periods. Table A-6 contains some example comparisons.

4. Statutes

Citation to statutes is virtually the same under the *Bluebook* and the *ALWD Manual.* Basic statutory citation rules are on pages 13 through 17 of the *Bluebook.*

Table A-6. Comparison of Selected Word Abbreviations in the
ALWD Manual and the *Bluebook*

Word	*ALWD Manual* (Appendix 3)	*Bluebook* (Table T.6)
Associate	Assoc.	Assoc.
Association	Assn.	Ass'n
Center	Ctr.	Ctr.
Commissioner	Commr.	Comm'r
Department	Dept.	Dep't
Hospital	Hosp.	Hosp.

5. *Signals and Parenthetical Information*

Introductory signals are covered on pages 4 through 5 of the *Blue-book*. The eighteenth edition of the *Bluebook* follows the same rule as the *ALWD Manual* on the use of the signal *see*: *see* is used only to show that the authority offers implicit support for an idea.

The rules for explanatory parentheticals are similar to those in the *ALWD Manual*. Under the *Bluebook* rule, parenthetical information generally should not be given in a complete sentence but should begin with a present participle (e.g., a verb ending in "-ing") that is not capitalized. BB 22-23, Rule B11.

6. *Quotations*

There is one slight difference in quotation rules: for the *Bluebook*, quotations that have fifty or more words must be set off in indented blocks. This means that the writer must count words to know exactly how many words the quotation contains. BB 23, Rule B12. In contrast, the *ALWD Manual* requires indented blocks for quotes that are fifty or more words *or* quotes that span four or more lines of typed text. ALWD 344, Rule 47.5(a).

7. *Tables in the* Bluebook

Pages with blue, vertical borders at the back of the *Bluebook* contain tables, BB 193-379, with information similar to that given in *ALWD Manual* appendices, ALWD 359-540. In the first table, however, federal material comes before state material; in the *ALWD Manual* that material comes at the end of the first appendix.

8. *Comparison of Arizona Citations in* ALWD *and* Bluebook *Formats*

Table A-7 shows examples of the common legal citations used in legal memoranda and court documents. These examples are given in both *ALWD* and *Bluebook* format.

Table A-7. Comparison of Arizona Citations
in *ALWD Manual* and *Bluebook* Formats

Source	*ALWD* Format	*Bluebook* Format (practice documents)
Arizona Constitution provision	Ariz. Const. art. 9, § 9.	Ariz. Const. art. 9, § 9.
Arizona statute	Ariz. Rev. Stat. Ann. § 17-363 (2004).	Ariz. Rev. Stat. Ann. § 17-363 (2004).
Arizona agency rule	Ariz. Admin. Code § 9-6-708 (2006).	Ariz. Admin. Code § 9-6-708 (2006).
Case from Arizona Supreme Court	*Nielson v. Patterson,* 204 Ariz. 530, 533 (2003).	*Nielson v. Patterson,* 204 Ariz. 530, 533 (2003).
Case from Arizona Court of Appeals	*Harrington v. Pulte Home Corp.,* 211 Ariz. 241, 245 (Ariz. App. 1 Div. 2005).	*Harrington v. Pulte Home Corp.,* 211 Ariz. 241, 245 (Ariz. Ct. App. 2005).

B. *Bluebook* Citations for Law Review Articles

Law review articles place citations in footnotes or endnotes, instead of placing citations in the main text of the document. BB 56, Rule 2.2. Most law review footnotes include text in ordinary type, in italics, and in large and small capital letters. This convention is not universal, and each law review selects the typefaces it will use. Some law reviews may use only ordinary type and italics. Others may use just ordinary type. BB 54–56, Rule 2.1.

The typeface used for a case name depends on (1) whether the case appears in the main text of the article or in a footnote and (2) how the case is used. When a case name appears in the main text of the article or in a textual sentence or footnote, it is italicized. By contrast, if a footnote contains an embedded citation, the case name is written in ordinary text. Similarly, when a full citation is given in a footnote, the case name is written in ordinary type. But when a short citation is used in footnotes, the case name is italicized. If submitting an article to a law review that uses all three typefaces, *Bluebook* Rule 2 dictates which typeface to use for each type of authority.

Law review footnotes use short citations generally the same as other documents. The short citation *id.* can be used only if the preceding footnote contains only one authority. BB 64, Rule 4.1. One unique *Bluebook* requirement is the "rule of five." This rule states that a short citation *id.* can only be used if the source is "*readily found in one of the preceding five footnotes.*" BB 97, Rule 10.9 (cases) (emphasis in original); BB 113, Rule 12.9 (statutes).

III. Editing Citations

To be sure that the citations in a document correctly reflect your research and support your analysis, include enough time in the writing and editing process to check citation accuracy. When writing the document, refer frequently to the citation guide required by your office or class. After the writing of the text of the document is finished, check the citations carefully again. Be sure that each citation is still accurate after all the writing revisions have been made. For example, moving a sentence might require you to change an *id.* to another form of short citation, or vice versa. In fact, some careful writers do not insert *id.* citations until they are completely finished writing and revising.

Sometimes editing for citations can take as long as editing for writing mechanics. The time invested in citations is well spent if it enables the person reading the document to quickly find the authorities cited and to understand the legal analysis.

Appendix B

Glossary of Legal Research Terms

Administrative Law is the general term for rules and decisions promulgated by state and federal agencies.

Advance Sheet is a soft-bound booklet that publishes the text of cases before they are published in a reporter.

Annotated Code is a code that contains extra research features for each statute, such as notes on the statute's history as well as citations to relevant attorney general opinions, West digest key numbers, treatises, forms, and secondary sources; it also provides cross-references to other relevant laws, including uniform laws.

Annotation is a generic term for an extra research feature of some constitutional and statutory compilations, for example, to provide citations to relevant cases or secondary sources. An annotation is also the name of an article in the *American Law Reports*.

Appellant is the party bringing the appeal in an intermediate appellate court.

Appellee is the party defending an appeal in an intermediate appellate court.

Bill Tracking is researching a statute in the current legislative session that has not yet been enacted.

Boolean Search is a search using specific connectors and commands to tell the search engine how the words and phrases should appear in a relevant source.

Case is a court's written opinion or decision. Each case explains a court's decision in a particular dispute.

Case Dates are the dates in a case providing information about when important procedural events occurred in the case.

Citation is a reference to an authority used to develop a legal argument and support a conclusion. A citation's information is used to locate the authority.

Citation Clause is a reference to an authority that supports a portion of a sentence and is placed immediately after that portion. A citation clause is set off from the sentence with commas.

Citation Sentence is a reference to an authority that supports an entire sentence and is placed after the sentence. A citation sentence begins with a capital letter and ends with a period.

Citator is a service that lists and analyzes citations to primary and secondary sources in other primary and secondary sources.

Common Law is judge-made law.

Concurring Opinion is the opinion written by a judge who agrees with the outcome of the majority opinion but for different reasons than those cited in the majority opinion.

Court Information is that part of a case that provides the full name of the court and any division or department that decided the case.

Court Rules are the instructions for doing anything in court, from filing a complaint to garnishing someone's wages.

Defendant is the defending party in a lawsuit.

Descriptive Word Index is a several-volume index organized by legal subjects; it is generally located at the beginning or end of a digest set. West publishes the Descriptive Word Index.

Digest is a set of books that organizes case summaries by topic or subject, instead of chronologically.

Disposition is the procedural conclusion of a case.

Dissenting Opinion is the opinion written by the judge who disagrees with the majority opinion.

Docket Number is the number assigned to a particular case by the deciding court.

En Banc is the term used to indicate that all judges of a court heard a case.

Enabling Act is the law that sets forth the explicit powers of an agency.

Federal Indian Law is the law dealing primarily with the status of the Indian tribes and their special relationship to the federal government.

Headnote is the short summary of an important legal principle discussed in a case. A headnote operates like a table of contents to a case and is located at the start of the case before the opinion begins. It has no precedential value.

Jump Cite is the citation to the exact page in the case that contains the idea being cited. See also "pinpoint cite."

Key Number is an actual number assigned by West to a sub-division of a large topic. Key numbers are part of the West digest system.

Legal Citation is a reference to an authority used to develop a legal argument and support a conclusion. A citation's information is used to locate the authority.

Legal Encyclopedia is similar to a general encyclopedia. It contains an alphabetical listing of legal topics and provides a general overview of the law for each topic.

Legal Periodicals are legal publications including legal newspapers, legal magazines, commercially published law journals, peer-edited law journals, and law-school published law journals (also commonly called law reviews). Some legal periodicals publish analytical articles on a narrow issue of law or a new area of law.

Legislative History is the compilation of documents created as a bill was considered by the legislature. Legislative history also refers to researching the events leading up to the passage of an enacted statute.

Majority Opinion is the opinion in a case that at least half of the judges support.

Mandatory Authority is authority that is binding on the court that would decide a conflict if the situation were litigated.

Natural Language means a search that is simply a question or phrase typed into the website's or database's search engine.

Official Code is a statutory code that a government or its designee publishes.

Official Reporter is a case reporter that a government or its designee publishes.

Parallel Citation is a citation to another reporter in which the case is also published.

Per Curiam is a term that means the court, rather than an individual judge, is the author of an opinion, although the court is made up of several judges.

Persuasive Authority is non-mandatory authority that a court has discretion to follow if the authority is relevant and well reasoned.

Petition for Certiorari is the document a party files if the party wishes the U.S. Supreme Court to hear a case.

Petitioner is the party bringing an appeal in the highest appellate court.

Pinpoint Cite is the citation to the exact page in the case that contains the idea being cited. See also "jump cite."

Plaintiff is the party bringing a lawsuit.

Plurality Opinion is the opinion with the most support that will decide the case, assuming no majority of judges supports an opinion.

Pocket Part is a soft-bound pamphlet that updates material in print media. Pocket parts are generally located inside the back cover of a book or directly on the shelf behind a book.

Primary Authority is law produced by government bodies with law-making power. Examples include constitutions, statutes, judicial opinions, and administrative agency rules. Primary authority can be either mandatory or persuasive authority, depending on the jurisdiction.

Regional Reporter is the case reporter published by West that includes cases from several states.

Regulation is the term used to label the law created by federal agencies and by some state agencies. See also "rule."

Reporter is a book that contains cases from a jurisdiction (or several jurisdictions) or on a particular topic in which the cases are arranged chronologically.

Research Terms are the comprehensive list of words, terms, and phrases that may lead to law on point when used to search indexes or to craft online word searches; these words, terms, and phrases commonly describe the client's situation.

Respondent is the party defending an appeal in the highest appellate court.

Rule is the term used to label law created by some state agencies. Arizona uses the term rule to refer to its agencies' laws. See also "regulation."

Secondary Authority is any legal source that is not primary authority. Secondary authority is designed to aid lawyers in understanding the law and locating primary authority. Examples include treatises, law review articles, and legal encyclopedias.

Synopsis is the short summary of the case that precedes the opinion. It has no precedential value.

Topic is a broad subject heading assigned by West to a broad legal principle in a case. Topics are part of the West digest system.

Topical Reporter is a reporter that publishes cases on a specific subject.

Treatise is a book about a legal topic.

Tribal Law is the law that Indian tribes use to govern themselves as sovereign bodies.

Unannotated Code is a code that contains only the text of the statutes; it does not include any extra research features, such as references to cases or secondary sources.

Unofficial Code is a code that a commercial company publishes without being designated by the state.

Unofficial Reporter is a reporter that a commercial company publishes without being designated by the state.

About the Author

Tamara S. Herrera is a Clinical Professor of Law at Sandra Day O'Connor College of Law at Arizona State University. She holds a Masters of Information and Library Science from the University of Arizona and a Juris Doctor from the University of Nebraska School of Law. She was an attorney with the law firm Ryley, Carlock & Applewhite before beginning her career in academia.

Index